Recipes for Memorable Gatherings

enjoy

PERLA SERVAN-SCHREIBER

Photography by Nathalie Carnet

Flammarion

"The more I give to thee,
The more I have ..."

Shakespeare, *Romeo and Juliet*

contents

Preface

ENJOY! It's MY word. It conveys delight and kindness and I've used it as my sign-off to emails and text messages for years. Intrinsically, it encompasses "joy".

Two gifts demonstrate my longtime affection for this word. The first is a sign spelling it out in big wooden letters that my "partner-in-crime" Sophie gave to me. It adorns my kitchen in Provence and welcomes everyone who enters. Before that, my team at *Psychologies* magazine, which I ran with my husband JL until 2008, gave me a T-shirt bearing my favorite sign-off.

So it was inevitable that "Enjoy" would one day rise through the ranks to become a title in its own right, and it's a perfect fit for this celebratory book.

I don't know if joy and enjoyment can be learned in the same way as we learn, say, geography, but I doubt it—if so, there would be more joyful people in the world. I do know that joy is contagious, that it feels good, and can change the lives of ourselves and those we love. So, steer clear of grinches and surround yourself instead with those who approach life with joy.

Whether it's summer or winter, I love gathering family, friends, and my friends' friends around a table because, when the food is good, joy naturally follows. The body and soul are in harmony and lasting memories are made.

It was through such "great gatherings" and the joy they brought that the idea for this book was born.

When you prepare food with your heart, even if you only cook occasionally, soups become merry, vegetables sing, salads dance, vinaigrettes laugh, and your children, loved ones, and friends will cook up their own memories and ask for more.

I draw inspiration from my Mediterranean roots, from France—my adopted home—and from my travels in Asia. I avoid junk food, but spoil myself with small treats every day—in moderation, if possible! I buy organic, but am not obsessive about it, and I often find myself snapping pictures of homemade bread or brioche fresh from the oven to share with my foodie friends. As soon as I set a big table, the party begins. I can already hear the laughter.

*I draw inspiration from
my Mediterranean roots.*

*I spoil myself with small treats
every day—in moderation,
if possible!*

Constraints stimulate creativity.

My mystery
ingredient is joy.

We spend at least as
much time laughing
as we spend working.

Introduction

Cooking with Joy

Finally the foodie era has arrived! For too long a "has-been," I'm now in tune with the times, as more and more of us find pleasure in cooking. When the world ground to a halt due to the global pandemic, cooking emerged as a welcome respite to the homebound everywhere—an unexpected silver lining.

If you follow my lead, you will rejoice. Seeing my food-loving family and friends helping themselves to seconds is one of my greatest pleasures. As a child, something I loved more than anything was to peek inside pots bubbling on the stove. Now I love watching my guests do the same, breathing in the aromas of what is simmering inside and sometimes even taking a taste. For me that's pure happiness!

It is in this spirit that I host large gatherings around my table, inspired by the memories of my Moroccan childhood. I came from a large family and my mother was a talented cook, so I want to dedicate this book to them all.

You might say there are so many cookbooks already, and I agree. But to me, cooking is about sharing and I wanted to share the secrets of my most unforgettable meals with you—and to divulge my mystery ingredient, which is joy.

I nurture it as I spend hours cooking, entering a state of flow that dispels any feeling of fatigue. On the contrary, it gives me a charge of energy and a feeling of lightness.

My Secrets for Great Gatherings

When preparing a meal for many guests, getting the proportions of ingredients right can be tricky. Recipes don't always scale up easily for crowds and doubling or tripling quantities doesn't necessarily work, especially for things like spices. Yet for mysterious reasons, you can often divide a recipe for twelve by three to serve four people. This is what I invite you to do, so you can enjoy this book of my favorite recipes for parties large *and* small.

Once you've decided to host a meal for a lot of people, the two greatest obstacles are often the equipment and the sheer hard work involved. You may not own extra-large skillets or huge stockpots but the solution is to use two smaller pans of the same size. This can help ensure successful results, especially when baking.

As for the "chore" of preparing vegetables, my approach is simple: let the fun start in the kitchen with those guests who are eager to lend a hand. I have no shortage of recruits, starting with my grandchildren. Zach, for example, has been on tiramisu duty since he was twelve, while Penelope helps with the mayonnaise. As for Arthur, he steps in as chef, with Theo, fifteen, who is heading the same way. And Alma is just getting started. All my grandchildren cook at home from time to time.

My friends are no exception when it comes to having all hands on deck. This improvised "culinary workshop" takes a bit of organization and space—I'm lucky in that I have a relatively big kitchen. But what I love most of all is passing on what I've learned. It goes without saying that we spend at least as much time laughing as we spend working.

If you prefer to work alone—which I like to do as well—forget about what I've just suggested and, the day before, prepare a one-dish meal that can be reheated when your guests arrive. There are many such recipes in this book and your gathering will be just as joyful.

Large gatherings are fleeting moments so, ideally, hosts should be at the table as much as possible to fully enjoy their guests' company. I confess this is something I don't always succeed in doing, even when it is possible, but I think that's part of my heritage. My mother was rarely at the table with us and my grandmother never was. After clearing away the dishes, she would sit at the end of a large rectangular table in the living room and eat at her own aristocratic pace (very slowly). Something I still envy her for today.

The Seasons are Your Number One Ally

In summer, having a kitchen garden is the ultimate luxury as it will decide the menu for you. But local farmers' markets are also an excellent place to start. For lunch, serve as a complete meal a selection of Middle Eastern-inspired salads made from vegetables, grains, proteins (optional), and plenty of fresh herbs. Chilled cucumber, tomato, or melon soups are also easy to prepare and guaranteed to be popular. All you need is a good blender and several no-fail recipes up your sleeve.

Something else you can't go wrong with is pasta and it's an easy way to make everyone, whatever their age, happy. In this book I've included my favorite big-batch pasta dishes with toppings such as curried summer squash, fresh tomatoes and basil, or caramelized onions and pancetta.

During winter, root vegetables, winter squash, and cruciferous vegetables like cauliflower and broccoli take center stage in warming soups or main dishes accompanied by different types of rice or grains such as quinoa, barley, or spelt (always organic).

The vegetarians in my life invite me to use my imagination—constraints stimulate creativity—but as you will see, nothing is demonized at my table, whether eggs, fish, or meat. Like many of you, we're flexitarians at my house and we deeply appreciate slow-cooked meats and stews like pot-au-feu that warm you from the inside out.

*Cooking and serving food
are the cornerstones of my
personal ecology.*

Whatever the season, the aperitif is a ritual beloved by all.
In these pages, you'll find many original ideas for cocktail hour,
including an addictive ginger and lemongrass infusion that is
drunk hot in winter and chilled in summer. A generous selection
of zakuska (hors d'oeuvres) has the added advantage that the
main meal can be simple, such as a good risotto (my current
obsession) and a salad. Dessert, of course, is a given.

Teatime is also sacred in my family (my husband and I forgo
lunch for our afternoon tea) and I've included a number of
homemade treats to honor this time of day.

Cooking as Meditation

Now that you know me better, I'll let you in on a secret: cooking
and serving food are the cornerstones of my personal ecology.
They make me happy and are a form of spirituality that fuels me
with silence and energy.

　　To me, preparing food and sharing it with loved ones
is a kind of active meditation that refocuses and calms me.
Discussing the evening's menu each morning with my husband
is a shared ritual that never fails to inspire me.

　　Cooking is magical—much more than a way to simply
nourish ourselves—it can strengthen old bonds or forge new
ones, build a family, and provide our grandchildren with
memories that someday they too will pass on.

　　It's impossible not to notice that, despite the foodie craze,
we are cooking less and less and, as a result, we are missing
out on the pleasures inherent in this ancient craft and the act

Cooking is magical—much more than a way to simply nourish ourselves—it can strengthen old bonds or forge new ones.

of handing it down to future generations. We're also eating increasingly poorly, and, even more troubling, more frequently alone—in many cases at our computers (sometimes even by choice). Eating just anything is an attack on our bodies and eating without pleasure harms our soul. Eating mindlessly prevents us from feeling satiated, which can lead to obesity and threaten our health.

But I'm an optimist, and I can see that the younger generations, both boys and girls, have a greater awareness of the environment and more culinary curiosity than their immediate elders. They are keener to buy organic produce, to set foot in the kitchen, and they are aware that both their health and the planet are in danger. I feel fortunate to be witnessing this change.

In this era of junk food, when restaurants, delivery services, and processed ready-made meals make it possible to eat anywhere and at any hour without having to cook, it's time to give the activity a significance that is both new and ancient at the same time: let's honor the sacred dimension of gathering in joy around a table to celebrate food, the land that produced it, and friendship.

When I go into my kitchen and put on my white linen apron, I begin to breathe more calmly. As all mystics will tell you, joy and spirituality are intertwined.

Tasting joy is like discovering a star as it connects you with something greater than yourself and makes you more luminous, more generous, and more joyful.

ENJOY!

My Tips and Tricks

MY GOLDEN RULES IN THE KITCHEN

Be **exacting** (when selecting ingredients and tools), **well-informed** (read the recipe from start to finish before you begin), **organized** (gather all the ingredients and equipment you'll need for each recipe), **focused** (live the moment and enjoy the process as a form of meditation), **precise** (respect the cooking times the first time you make a recipe, particularly when baking, but keep in mind that ovens heat differently), **attentive, creative** (trust yourself, adjust the quantities to suit your taste, and then jot down any changes you make), and **adventurous** (try at least one new recipe a week).

SCALING RECIPES UP OR DOWN

All of the recipes in this book are designed to serve ten or twelve people but the quantities can easily be divided by three or four if you're feeding a smaller party. As a general rule, you should take care when scaling a recipe up as ingredients do not always rescale proportionally and the recipe may not work if you simply multiply the amounts of ingredients. Keep in mind that cooking times can vary when adjusting quantities.

USING THE TOOLS YOU HAVE TO FEED A CROWD

If you don't have large enough pots, pans, or molds to make the recipes in this book, use two of the same size and material to ensure the best results.

PREPARING SILICONE MOLDS

There is no need to grease a silicone mold with butter. Before adding dough or batter, run it under cold water and shake it over the sink to remove excess moisture; do not wipe it dry.

TWO SPATULAS ARE BETTER THAN ONE

As you will see, I recommend stirring with two wooden spatulas. It's far more efficient to stir mushrooms in a skillet or vegetables in a wok with two spatulas of the same size than just one.

Once you've tried it, the action becomes second nature. The same goes for tossing a salad—two utensils are better than one.

CHOOSING YOUR INGREDIENTS

Although it might sound obvious, the quality of your ingredients really does make a difference. For best results, use the finest ingredients you can get, either fresh or frozen, depending on the recipe, and preferably buy organic.

FILTERED WATER

I always recommend using filtered water, which typically has a more neutral taste than tap water; it helps to ensure that the flavor of your ingredients shines through, and this is particularly true for vegetables. However, if you don't have a special pitcher or filtering system, using tap water is perfectly fine.

GARLIC GERMS

Cut garlic cloves in half lengthwise and remove the germs, especially when the garlic is older and the germs have turned green and bitter. This step is particularly important when you'll be using the garlic raw or just lightly cooked.

BRING BAKING INGREDIENTS TO ROOM TEMPERATURE
When making pastries and cakes, your ingredients (particularly eggs) should be at cool room temperature, unless a recipe indicates otherwise. Plan ahead and take butter, milk, and eggs out of the refrigerator about an hour ahead of time, depending on the temperature in your kitchen.

FREEZER-FRIENDLY SOUPS
All the soups in this book that are to be served hot can be prepared, cooled, and then frozen for up to three months, so it's a good idea to double the recipe quantities and freeze portions in airtight containers for evenings when you don't have the time or desire to cook. Reheat the soup in a saucepan over low heat, or in the microwave, adjust the seasoning, and voilà, dinner is served! I recommend making double batches of My Chicken Broth (see p. 118) and freezing the excess so that you'll always have broth readily on hand for the recipes that call for stock or bouillon cubes.

VEGETARIAN AND GLUTEN-FREE OPTIONS
Many recipes in this book are suitable for vegetarians and there is an index on page 253 to help you to find those dishes that are veggie-friendly. You will also find many recipes that guests who are gluten intolerant will love (see p. 253).

MEZE
I adore meze, the delicious eastern Mediterranean tradition of serving a selection of small dishes at the same time, often with Spiced Flatbread (see p. 216). Many of the dishes in this book can be served meze style, such as the Roasted Eggplant with Oregano and Balsamic (see p. 51), Smoky Eggplant Caviar (see p. 52), My Family's Shakshuka (see p. 58), Roasted Rainbow Bell Peppers (see p. 74), and Tabbouleh (see p. 49).

CHUTNEY STORAGE
I always like to have chutney on hand to serve with grilled meats, curries, and rice dishes such as Persian Basmati Rice (see p. 136) and Klima Indra (see p. 164–65). The chutneys on pages 166–69 can be stored in a sealed jar or an airtight container in the refrigerator (not the freezer) for about three months.

CONVERSIONS

Some Notes on Measuring

When making the recipes in this book, follow either the metric or imperial measurements (for consistency, avoid mixing the two). For best results, use digital scales (especially when baking) and, unless indicated otherwise, cup and spoon measures are level.

Oven Temperature Conversions

As individual ovens vary, the cooking times given should only be taken as a guide, particularly for baked recipes. The temperatures below are for conventional electric and gas ovens, for fan ovens check your manufacturer's guide.

Fahrenheit	250ºF	275ºF	300ºF	325ºF	350ºF	375ºF	400ºC	425ºF	450ºF	475ºF
Celsius	120°C	140°C	150°C	160°C	180°C	190°C	200°C	220°C	230°C	245°C
UK gas mark	½	1	2	3	4	5	6	7	8	9

Butter Equivalents

US standard	Imperial weight	Metric weight
1 tbsp	½ oz.	15 g
½ US stick (4 tbsp or ¼ cup)	2 oz.	60 g
1 US stick (8 tbsp or ½ cup)	4 oz.	115 g
2 US sticks (1 cup)	8 oz.	230 g

Liquid Measures

US standard	Practical metric equivalent
1 tsp	5 ml
1 tbsp	15 ml
¼ cup or 4 tbsp	60 ml
⅓ cup or 5 tbsp	75 ml
½ cup	125 ml
1 cup	250 ml

spring / summer

Chilled Soups

Salads

Vegetables

Pasta

Fish and Shellfish

Desserts

Chilled Cucumber Soup

If you like yogurt, you'll love this! Inspired by Indian raita (except you eat it with a spoon), it is refreshing and so pretty, making it the perfect starter for a lunch or dinner on a sweltering day. Stay in the shade, listen to the cicadas, and make this chilled soup. Cooling off doesn't get any simpler than this!

Times
Active: 25 minutes
Resting: 15 minutes
Chilling: 30 minutes

Serves 10
—

Ingredients
- 2 large cucumbers, 1¼ lb. (600 g) each
- 2 level tsp Guérande sea salt (or kosher salt)
- 1–1½ cups (9–13 oz./250– 375 g) plain whole milk yogurt
- 4 Roma tomatoes, 3½ oz. (100 g) each (optional)
- 6 scallions (optional)
- 10 walnut halves (optional)
- 3 tbsp finely chopped fresh cilantro
- 3 tbsp finely chopped fresh mint

Wash and peel the cucumbers, leaving a few strips of skin. Cut the cucumbers in half lengthwise, scoop out the seeds with a spoon, and slice thinly. Place the slices in a strainer set over a bowl to collect the juice. Sprinkle the cucumber with the salt, place a weight on top to press it down, and let it sit for 15 minutes so the excess liquid in it drains out.

Whisk the yogurt in a salad bowl until smooth and then stir in the cucumber juice. Rinse and drain the cucumber slices and mix them with the yogurt. Add more whisked yogurt if you'd like the soup to be thinner or, if you've used thick Greek yogurt, you may need to thin it with a little whole milk. Chill for 30 minutes.

Meanwhile, peel the tomatoes (if using) with a tomato or vegetable peeler. Cut them in half, remove the seeds, and dice finely. Rinse the scallions (if using) and slice thinly. Roughly chop the walnuts (if using).

When ready to serve, stir the cilantro and mint into the chilled soup. Serve at once with the optional tomatoes, scallions, and walnuts in separate bowls so guests may garnish their soup to taste.

Chickpea Gazpacho

If you can't face another tomato salad or gazpacho, but summer is not yet over, then try this. Thanks to the chickpeas, it's a kind of creamy gazpacho but is easier to digest without the bell peppers, and the salmon pink hue couldn't be prettier. Success depends on you having a good blender, as gaspachiche, as I call it, must be perfectly smooth. The origin of the dish? As I was writing this book, I came across a recipe scribbled in pencil on a little slip of paper saying, "gaspachiche—tomato, bell pepper, celery, vinegar, olive oil, and a few chickpeas," which I must have seen in a magazine. My first attempt—made without the peppers—was a hit, as all four of us eating it (myself included) agreed. Only one person commented there was a little too much vinegar, which wasn't off the mark, but that is a matter of taste. Give the recipe a try when tomatoes are at their most flavorful and feel free to experiment with the quantities to find your perfect combination.

Times

Active: 15 minutes
Chilling: 2 hours or longer

Serves 12
—

Ingredients

- 3½ lb. (1.5 kg) ripe, flavorful tomatoes, preferably Russian or beefsteak
- 3 celery stalks, plus 8 leaves
- 4 small scallions
- 1 new garlic clove
- Generous ½ cup (3 oz./80 g) cooked chickpeas (drained and rinsed, if canned)
- 6 tbsp extra-virgin olive oil
- 2 tbsp sherry vinegar
- Salt and freshly ground pepper

Wash and roughly chop the tomatoes, celery, and scallions. Peel the garlic, remove the germ, and roughly chop. Place all the ingredients in a blender, including the celery leaves, and blend on maximum speed for 4–5 minutes until perfectly smooth and creamy. Taste and adjust the seasoning, if necessary.

Cover and chill in the refrigerator for 2 hours, or longer if you prefer the soup very cold. It will also freeze. I usually serve the chickpea gazpacho in clear glasses, as in the photograph, but, for a striking contrast, I sometimes use dark red bowls.

Facing page, from left to right:
Melon Gazpacho with Chili (p. 36),
Yellow-Fleshed Melon Gazpacho with Chili (p. 36),
Pea Velouté or Green Gazpacho (p. 37),
and Chickpea Gazpacho (p. 22).

Melon Gazpacho with Chili

You may love melon in slices or cut up and eaten with a spoon, but it is also enjoyable and decidedly more original to "drink" it from time to time—especially when it's chilled and boldly seasoned, as in this recipe.

Times

Active: 30 minutes
Chilling: 2 hours or longer

Serves 12
—

Ingredients

- 6 perfectly ripe Charentais or Cantaloupe melons (or 2 large yellow- or orange-fleshed melons)
- 1 tsp *piment d'Espelette*
- 6 tbsp extra-virgin olive oil
- 4 tbsp sherry vinegar
- 20 basil leaves
- Salt and freshly ground pepper

Cut the melons in half and scrape out the seeds. Using a melon baller, scoop out small balls from one of the melons, and refrigerate until ready to serve.

Cut the flesh of the remaining melons into cubes and place one-quarter in a food processor, filling the bowl no more than two-thirds full. Add one-quarter each of the *piment d'Espelette*, olive oil, vinegar, and basil, and season with salt and pepper.

Process until perfectly smooth, taste for seasoning, and then transfer to a large soup tureen. Repeat the same process three more times until you have used up all the ingredients. Chill for at least 2 hours or until ready to serve. Check the seasoning again and adjust if necessary.

Serve in glasses or bowls with a few melon balls slipped into each serving.

Notes

You can play around with contrasting colors, such as adding watermelon balls or a few red currants to each serving. The eye and palate will be pleasantly surprised.

Pea Velouté or Green Gazpacho

Can you think of anything smoother and more addictive to eat than a creamy velouté? The great Freud would no doubt say it recalls our earliest memories of food. Serve this hot in winter, sprinkled with chervil, or chilled in summer. You can serve it all year if you use frozen vegetables, or in spring if you prefer fresh. It is one of my top five veloutés!

Times
Make a day ahead
Active: 10 minutes
Cooking: 30 minutes
Chilling: 2–8 hours (if serving cold)

Serves 10
—

Ingredients
- 2 onions
- 1 cucumber
- 1 bunch flat-leaf parsley
- 15 mint leaves
- 6⅓-8 cups (1½-2 liters) water
- 4 tbsp (2 oz./60 g) salted butter
- 1 handful chopped spinach leaves (or thawed frozen spinach or 1 lettuce heart)
- 2 lb. (1 kg) shelled fresh peas (or frozen)
- 1 tbsp agave syrup (or sugar)
- Salt and freshly ground pepper

To garnish (if serving hot)
- 1 handful chervil leaves

Peel the onions and cucumber and slice thinly. Wash and dry the parsley and mint and remove the parsley leaves from their stems. Bring the water to a boil in a large saucepan.

In another large saucepan, melt the butter over low heat. Add the onions and cucumber, cook for 1 minute, and then add the spinach (or lettuce), the mint, parsley, peas, and agave syrup (or sugar). Pour in about three-quarters of the boiling water, return to a boil, then reduce the heat to low, cover, and simmer for 30 minutes.

Turn off the heat, uncover the pan, and let the soup cool for 10 minutes before blending until perfectly smooth and creamy (do this in batches, if necessary). If the soup is too thick for your liking, add more of the water. Taste and add more salt, pepper, or mint if necessary.

If serving the velouté hot, reheat gently. Wash, dry, and chop the chervil, and sprinkle it over the soup before taking it to the table. If serving it cold, cover and refrigerate for at least 2 hours, or 8 hours if you want it very well chilled and wonderfully refreshing.

Vanilla-Scented Tomato and Strawberry Carpaccio

In the height of summer, when tomatoes and strawberries are at their best, I'm inspired to serve them together, and I also thought "why not add some vanilla?" This playful pairing of three contrasting flavors—two of which are usually more at home in desserts—makes for a deliciously unusual starter.

Times

Active: 30 minutes
Infusing: 1 hour (or overnight)

Serves 10
—

Ingredients

- 2 Madagascan or Tahitian vanilla beans (or 1 tsp ground vanilla bean)
- 5 tbsp extra-virgin olive oil
- 10 tomatoes (see Notes)
- 15–20 small, sweet strawberries (depending on size), such as Mara des Bois
- Juice of 3 lemons (or 4 tbsp white vinegar)
- Fleur de sel and freshly ground pepper

Split the vanilla beans lengthwise and scrape out the seeds into a bowl (or add the ground vanilla, if using, to the bowl). Spoon the olive oil over the seeds and let infuse for at least 1 hour. If you have time, overnight is even better.

Peel the tomatoes and slice them into even rounds. Divide between two serving dishes.

Wash and hull the strawberries and slice them thinly from top to bottom. Arrange over the tomatoes.

Just before serving the carpaccio, drizzle over half the vanilla-infused oil and all of the lemon juice or vinegar, but do not mix. Season with fleur de sel and pepper and drizzle with the rest of the vanilla oil. Serve immediately and be prepared for an explosion of flavors with every mouthful.

Notes

My favorite tomato to eat raw is the large, vividly red, meaty Russian variety.

Pearl Barley, Mushroom, and Herb Salad

This recipe is the perfect opportunity to start a party in your kitchen with your friends. The chore of chopping herbs and slicing mushrooms becomes fun and you'll be rewarded by the wonderful flavors of a dressing inspired by Ottolenghi.

Times
Active: 2 hours (if preparing alone; 1 hour if there are two of you)
Soaking: 1–2 hours
Cooking: 10 minutes
Marinating: 2 hours

Serves 12
—

Ingredients
- 1¾ cups (12 oz./350 g) pearl barley

For the dressing
- 6 shallots
- 3 tbsp soft brown sugar
- 2 tbsp best-quality sherry vinegar

For the salad
- 1 crisp celery heart with its yellow inner leaves
- 2¾ lb. (1.25 kg) firm white button mushrooms
- Juice of 1 lemon
- 4½ oz. (120 g) flat-leaf parsley (about 3 large bunches)
- 1 oz. (30 g) tarragon leaves (about 2 bunches)
- 6–8 tbsp olive oil
- Seeds of 2 pomegranates (or 9 oz./250 g red currants)
- Guérande sea salt (or kosher salt) and freshly ground black pepper

To prepare and cook the pearl barley, rinse the barley under cold water and place it in a bowl. Cover with fresh cold water and let soak for 1–2 hours. It's not essential to soak the barley, but if you don't, the cooking time will be longer (about 25 minutes). Bring a saucepan of water to a boil, drain the barley and add it to the saucepan. Bring the water back to a boil, lower the heat, and let cook for 10 minutes. The barley grains must be tender but still have a little bite. Drain the barley in a strainer, run cold water over it, and let cool.

Prepare the dressing 2 hours before serving. Peel and finely chop the shallots. In a bowl, whisk the sugar and vinegar together until the sugar has completely dissolved. Add the shallots and set aside to marinate until ready to serve.

To prepare the salad, wash and finely slice the celery stalks and leaves. Wipe the mushrooms, slice them as thinly as possible, and toss in the lemon juice until coated. Wash and chop the parsley and tarragon leaves. Place the barley in a salad bowl, add the lemon-dressed mushrooms, chopped parsley, tarragon, and olive oil to taste. Season with salt and freshly ground black pepper. Mix everything together until combined and scatter over the pomegranate seeds or red currants. Finally, pour over the dressing that has been marinating. Taste, add more vinegar if necessary, and serve.

Notes
Be generous with the herbs, as indicated in the recipe. In fact, be generous with everything, as this salad brings on a kind of amnesia—you'll forget you already had three helpings!

Lebanese Red Onion and Parsley Salad

Don't shy away, as I once did, from this oniony salad as not only is it surprisingly sweet, but it is also beautifully crisp. I first tasted it in a restaurant in Beirut and ever since I've been searching for the perfect harmony of flavors that the Lebanese are so gifted at creating. Well, here it is. It'll bring tears to your eyes, but they'll be tears of joy!

Times

Active: 20 minutes
Resting: 10 minutes

Serves 10
—

Ingredients

- 5 or 6 red onions
  (or a combination of red and
  white), depending on size
- 1 large bunch flat-leaf parsley
- 25 mint leaves
- 2 tbsp ground sumac
- Juice of 2 lemons
- 3 tbsp extra-virgin olive oil
- Fleur de sel

To serve (optional)
- Pita bread or Spiced Flatbread
  (see recipe p. 216–17)
- Assorted meze (see Notes)

Peel and thinly slice the onions. Wash and dry the parsley and finely chop the leaves. Wash, dry, and finely chop the mint, reserving a few leaves for garnish.

Place the onions in a large salad bowl and sprinkle with the sumac and a little fleur de sel. Stir to mix.

Add the parsley, mint, lemon juice, and olive oil and stir well. Taste and add more salt or lemon juice if needed.

Let rest for 10 minutes, scatter over the reserved mint leaves, and enjoy.

Notes

In Lebanon, this salad is typically served as part of a meze spread and is loved by visitors and locals alike. Don't hesitate to recreate this tasty tradition at home, surrounding the salad with Smoky Eggplant Caviar (see recipe p. 52), My Family's Shakshuka (see recipe p. 58–59) without the poached eggs, and Tabbouleh (see recipe p. 49). The traditional accompaniment is pita bread, as it is so handy for scooping up meze with your fingers, but Spiced Flatbread is equally good.

Red and Green Detox Salad

—

This was a real discovery during my annual stay at the Buchinger Wilhelmi clinic, where you can choose to follow a liquid-based therapeutic fast or a calorie-reduced diet of 800 or 1,000 calories a day, according to your doctor's recommendations. My stay includes at least two hours of exercise every day and, after ten days, I always feel lighter, with my mind clear and full of ideas. Pairing refreshing red watermelon with green celery, both of which are diuretic, is genius. Not only is the combination delicious, it is also very healthy and 100 percent guilt-free. You can dress the salad with a drizzle of flaxseed oil, walnut oil, and lemon juice, or an avocado sauce sharpened with lemon and diluted with a little water to make it more liquid. I personally like to add herbs, a drizzle of walnut oil, and that's all. It's worth noting this salad as a way of combining fruits and vegetables, which we don't do often enough. Fennel and orange are another match made in heaven.

Red and Green Detox Salad

Times

Active: 45 minutes

Serves 10
—

Ingredients

- 1 large or 2 small bunches celery, with firm, crisp stalks and vibrant green leaves
- 1 large slice of watermelon per person
- 2 ripe avocados
- 3 tbsp finely chopped flat-leaf parsley (or another herb of your choice)
- 1 tbsp extra-virgin olive oil (or walnut oil)
- Juice of 2 lemons (or 2 tsp balsamic vinegar)
- Salt and freshly ground pepper

To serve
- Pumpkin seeds

To clean the celery, separate the stalks, including the tender inner ribs, and cut off the leaves. Rinse the stalks and a handful of leaves quickly under cold running water and dry thoroughly. Using a vegetable peeler, strip away the coarser strings from the stalks, which are unpleasant to eat. Slice the stalks thinly and shred the leaves. Peel the watermelon and cut the flesh into small dice. Halve the avocados and pit, peel, and dice the flesh.

In a salad bowl, combine the diced watermelon and sliced celery.

To make the avocado dressing, place the avocados, parsley (or herb of your choice), and oil in a blender. Measure the amount of lemon juice you've squeezed and add it (or the balsamic vinegar, if using) to the blender with an equal quantity of water. Season with salt and pepper and blend until smooth. Taste and add more salt, pepper, or lemon juice (or vinegar) as needed. Transfer the dressing to a bowl and serve on the side for guests to help themselves. Just before serving, sprinkle with pumpkin seeds for added nutrients and a little extra crunch.

Tabbouleh

Everyone thinks they are familiar with this Lebanese specialty, which is essentially a parsley salad combined with a little fresh tomato and bulgur. However, in the West, we've managed to reverse the traditional proportions of ingredients so the bulgur and tomato are dominant, while the parsley plays a supporting role. That is not tabbouleh, but rather a bulgur and tomato salad, so let's give real tabbouleh a whirl. Enlist the help of your friends, children, and neighbors as, if you're feeding a crowd, you'll need them to wash, dry, de-stem, and finely chop an impressive amount of parsley. My philosophy? Joy starts by coming together in the kitchen and from there moves to the table, where it creates lifelong memories. Just ask my grandchildren.

Times

Active: about 45 minutes, depending on how many helpers you have in the kitchen
Soaking: 1 hour

Serves 10
—

Ingredients

- ¾ cup (3½ oz./100 g) coarse bulgur
- 6 bunches flat-leaf parsley
- 3 small white onions
- 6 Roma tomatoes
- Juice of 4 lemons
- 4–5 tbsp extra-virgin olive oil
- 1 tbsp sumac (optional)
- Salt and freshly ground pepper

To serve (see Notes)
- Roasted Eggplant with Oregano and Balsamic (see recipe p. 51)

Soak the bulgur in warm water for 1 hour until softened.
Wash and dry the parsley and finely chop the leaves. Peel and finely chop the onions, wash and dry the tomatoes, and cut both into small dice. Drain the bulgur, place it in a salad bowl, and top with the parsley, onions, and tomatoes.
All this preparation can be done several hours in advance, but only season the tabbouleh when you are ready to serve it. Just before taking it to the table, add the lemon juice, olive oil, salt, and pepper. Stir to combine, then taste and adjust the seasoning. Sprinkle with sumac (if using), and serve at once.

Notes

You can serve this tabbouleh on its own or with a selection of other salads. I'm assuming you will also offer the Roasted Eggplant with Oregano and Balsamic (see recipe p. 51).

Roasted Eggplant with Oregano and Balsamic

This Italian-inspired recipe is radically different from the following one of Lebanese origin, but it is equally addictive and even easier to make. Another advantage is you can prepare it ahead and it works just as well whether you are cooking for four or for twelve. There is one caveat, however—this dish is best in summer, when eggplants are at their peak. Besides those from my garden, I particularly like the plump, round ones from Sicily as they are packed with flavor. Striped eggplants, sweeter than their purple cousins, are also good, but no matter which variety you use, make sure they are firm and shiny and their stems are very green.

Times

Active: 20 minutes
Cooking: 10–15 minutes, using two ovens
Resting: 2–3 hours

Serves 12
—

Ingredients

- Extra-virgin olive oil
- 12 eggplants (or 6 large Sicilian eggplants)
- 5 tbsp dried oregano (or more to taste)
- Scant 1 cup (225 ml) balsamic vinegar
- Kosher salt and freshly ground pepper

Preheat the ovens to the highest possible temperature on fan setting.

Brush two rimmed baking sheets (or shallow roasting pans) with olive oil and sprinkle with a little kosher salt. Rinse and dry the eggplants and cut off the stems. Cut into ⅔-in. (1.5-cm) slices and place them on the baking sheets. Place one baking sheet in the center of each oven.

Roast the eggplants for 10–15 minutes until golden and lightly browned. Roast the second batch. Arrange the slices in layers on serving dishes and sprinkle with the oregano. Season with freshly ground pepper and drizzle generously with ½ cup (125 ml) of the balsamic vinegar, followed by a drizzle of olive oil. Let rest for 2–3 hours at room temperature, adding more vinegar and oil as needed, if the eggplant has fully absorbed them.

Just as the eggplant drinks up the vinegar, your guests will devour these golden-brown, melt-in-the-mouth eggplant slices.

Smoky Eggplant Caviar

Another irresistible meze dish in the Lebanese tradition. This smoky eggplant caviar can be served with other Middle Eastern-inspired starters or as a side for grilled meat or fish, in which case double the quantities. For once, I'm counting on you to properly char your eggplants and not remove them from the oven too soon, even if your neighbors smell something burning!

Times

Active: 45 minutes
Cooking: 30 minutes
Draining: 10–30 minutes

Serves 10
—

Ingredients

- 6 large eggplants, preferably round Sicilian ones
- 1 bunch flat-leaf parsley
- 1 bunch mint
- 5 lemons
- 6 large pink garlic cloves
- 5 tbsp extra-virgin olive oil
- 2 tbsp light tahini
- 2 tbsp ground cumin
- 1 tbsp sumac
- Salt and freshly ground pepper

To serve (optional)
- Seeds of 1 pomegranate

Preheat the oven to the highest possible temperature on fan setting.

Line a rimmed baking sheet with aluminum foil. Wash the eggplants, pierce them in several places with the tip of a paring knife, and set them whole on the baking sheet. Roast them for about 30 minutes, turning them over two or three times during cooking.

While the eggplants are cooking, wash and dry the parsley and mint, and chop the leaves finely. Grate the zest of two of the lemons into a bowl, juice all five lemons, and combine the juice and zest.

Once the eggplants are well charred, remove them from the oven. When they are cool enough to handle, cut them in half lengthwise and scrape out the flesh with a spoon, discarding any bits of skin. Place the flesh in a strainer for at least 10 minutes to let excess liquid drain out. Meaty Sicilian eggplants contain very little water so they do not need to drain for long, but other varieties may need to be left in the strainer for up to 30 minutes.

Transfer the eggplant flesh to a large salad bowl. Peel the garlic, removing the germs, crush, and add with the lemon juice and zest, olive oil, tahini, parsley, mint, and cumin. Season with salt and pepper and mix with a fork for a good 5 minutes until well combined. Taste and adjust the seasoning as necessary.

Just before serving, stir in the sumac, top with the pomegranate seeds (if using), and enjoy.

Caponata

In my opinion, caponata is one of Italy's finest traditional dishes. Whether I serve it chilled or at room temperature, it's always a winner. Although cooked in oil, it is not heavy and it's packed with sweet-sour flavors; if you leave the celery a bit crisp, there are contrasting textures when you eat it. Best of all, you can make caponata a day ahead.

Times
Active: 15 minutes
Cooking: 35–40 minutes

Serves 12
—

Ingredients
- 3 lb. (1.5 kg) eggplants
- 8 firm, crisp celery stalks with leaves
- 4 lb. (1.8 kg) firm, meaty tomatoes
- 1 lb. (500 g) white or yellow onions
- 4 tbsp extra-virgin olive oil, plus extra for greasing
- 4 tbsp tomato paste
- ½ cup (120 ml) red wine vinegar
- ⅓ cup (2½ oz./75 g) sugar
- Scant ½ cup (3 oz./80 g) capers or thinly sliced cornichons (optional)
- Salt and freshly ground pepper

Preheat the oven to the highest possible temperature. Brush a rimmed baking sheet with olive oil. Wash and dry the eggplants, cut off the stems, and remove the skin in alternating strips lengthwise. Cut into ½-in. (1-cm) dice and spread out in a single layer on the baking sheet.

Roast in the oven for 10–15 minutes until tender and golden. You have just saved 2 cups (500 ml) of oil by not frying the eggplants in a skillet! Wash and dry the celery and cut it into ½-in. (1-cm) slices. Bring a saucepan of water to a boil, add the celery, blanch for 2 minutes, and drain.

Peel the tomatoes, cut them in half, remove the seeds, and cut the flesh into small dice. Peel the onions and chop them finely. Heat the 4 tablespoons of olive oil in a large skillet or sauté pan over low heat. Add the onions and cook, stirring occasionally, until softened (about 10 minutes). Stir in the tomatoes and tomato paste and season with salt and pepper. Simmer for 10 minutes to let the tomatoes cook down. Add the vinegar, sugar, capers or cornichons (if using), eggplant, and celery. Stir and let simmer for several minutes to allow the sauce to thicken and the flavors to blend.

Taste and add more salt, pepper, or vinegar as needed— caponata should be intensely flavorful and piquant, but if you're not a big vinegar fan, there's no need to add more. Serve warm, at room temperature, or chilled.

Notes
You can serve caponata as a side for meat, poultry, or fish, but I particularly like it on its own as a starter.

My Family's Shakshuka
—

*There's a bit of Proust in all of us. That's his genius.
Shakshuka is one of many Judeo-Arabic specialties that
reflect the culinary fraternity between these two cultures,
which is evident in my own cooking and its Moroccan
roots. The basic recipe is always the same: slow-cooked bell
peppers, tomatoes, garlic, and olive oil, but the variations—
between countries, families, and available spices—are
endless. My own family's version was simple. We'd have
shakshuka as a starter on Shabbat only, starting Friday
evening, served with several other small dishes (or meze)
made with vegetables such as carrots, eggplants, beets,
chard, radishes, and raw fennel. The homemade bread
was always fresh and wonderful, so we'd gorge ourselves
on bread and "salads," as we called them, and often would
have no room for the traditional fish course that followed.
On Fridays, I'd get home from school at around 4 p.m., just
as our bread was being delivered warm from the public
ovens. The shakshuka would be nearing the end of its
simmering time and on the best days it was just beginning
to stick to the bottom of the pan—a sign it was perfectly
cooked. Unlike my school friends, my favorite after-school
snack was no longer bread with chocolate spread, but a
sandwich of caramelized shakshuka that I had scraped off
the bottom of the pan and spread on fresh sesame bread.
Shakshuka is my madeleine.*

My Family's Shakshuka

Times

Active: 1 hour
Cooking: 2½–3½ hours (see Notes)

Serves 12
—

Ingredients

- 6 large bell peppers (2 green, 2 red, and 2 yellow, unless, like me, you can only digest the red ones)
- 11 lb. (5 kg) large, ripe tomatoes (see Notes)
- 12 pink garlic cloves
- 1 cup (250 ml) extra-virgin olive oil
- 4 tbsp sweet paprika
- 2 tbsp ground cumin
- ½ tsp Cayenne pepper (optional)
- 3 tbsp sugar
- 4 tbsp white vinegar
- 12 eggs (optional) (see Notes)
- Salt and freshly ground pepper

To serve
- Freshly baked Kesra (see recipe p. 225), or another good artisan bread

Preheat the oven to the highest possible temperature. Line a rimmed baking sheet with parchment paper.

When the oven is really hot, roast the bell peppers whole on the baking sheet for about 15 minutes, until the skin, but not the flesh, is charred all over.

Transfer the peppers to a strainer in the sink and run cold water over them until they are cool enough to peel off the skins. Cut the peppers in half, remove the seeds, and slice into thin strips.

Peel the tomatoes and cut them into small dice. If there are a lot of seeds, first cut the tomatoes in half and press lightly in the palm of your hand to remove the seeds, before cutting into small dice.

Peel six of the garlic cloves, removing the germs and leaving the rest whole and unskinned. Heat the oil in a large Dutch oven (see Notes) over medium-high heat and add the paprika, cumin, Cayenne (if using), sugar, tomatoes, bell peppers, vinegar, and garlic. Season with salt and pepper and heat until bubbling, stirring nonstop with two spatulas.

Lower the heat to medium and cook, stirring occasionally, for 2–3 hours until the mixture is very thick and beginning to caramelize. Leave in the whole garlic cloves as there are always garlic lovers among the guests. Now is the time to add the eggs (see Notes).

Shakshuka is best served hot, but it's also delicious warm or at room temperature. The dish isn't complete without good bread, though, preferably freshly baked Kesra.

Notes

If your tomatoes are large, meaty, and contain little water, you can sauté the ingredients in two skillets over high heat in two pans, instead of caramelizing them slowly for 2 hours. Once the liquid has evaporated sufficiently, the dish will be ready in 30 minutes.
If you crave shakshuka in winter, avoid the tomatoes sold in supermarkets, as they will be full of water, replacing them with frozen or canned chopped tomatoes, preferably Italian.
To serve with poached eggs, cook shakshuka in two large skillets or, if you've only used one pan, divide the mixture between two skillets once it is cooked, and reheat when ready to serve. Using a ladle, make six indentations in each pan, equally spaced apart, and crack an egg into each. Cover the pans and cook over medium heat until the egg whites are set but the yolks are still runny. Remove from the heat and serve straight away.
Shakshuka can be served as an appetizer or as a main dish accompanied by a green salad.

Zucchini Clafoutis

I couldn't tell you how many times I've made this clafoutis, or how many times I've given the recipe to friends who have asked for it as soon as they've had a taste. When you do something that makes you happy, you stop counting! Although zucchini and basil are available all year round, this dish is best in the summer when both are at their peak. I can't think of a better lunch on a hot day, served with a large salad on the side, with everyone gathered around a table in the shade.

Times

Active: 30 minutes
Cooking: 30 minutes

Serves 12
—

Ingredients

- 6 tbsp extra-virgin olive oil
- 2½ lb. (1.2 kg) zucchini
- 4 new garlic cloves
- Leaves from 1 bunch basil
- 12 eggs
- 2 pinches freshly grated nutmeg
- 3 tbsp finely chopped flat-leaf parsley
- 2 tbsp white bread crumbs
- 1 cup (3½ oz./100 g) finely grated Parmesan
- Salt and freshly ground pepper

Preheat the oven to 300°F (150°C/Gas mark 2). Grease two 9-in. (22-cm) round baking dishes (preferably porcelain) with a little of the olive oil.

Wash the zucchini and cut off the ends. Grate, using a food processor fitted with the coarse shredding disk or on the large holes of a box grater. Peel the garlic, remove the germs, and finely chop. Wash, dry, and finely chop the basil.

Set two large skillets over high heat. When they are hot, add the rest of the olive oil and zucchini. Sauté for 3 minutes, stirring often, until softened but not golden. Season lightly with salt and then remove from the heat.

Whisk the eggs in a large bowl with a fork. Whisk in the nutmeg and season with salt and pepper. Take the skillets off the heat, add the garlic, basil, and parsley to the zucchini, and stir for 30 seconds. Add the bread crumbs and stir for 30 seconds more.

Return the skillets to the burners and reduce the heat to medium-low. Divide the eggs equally between the skillets and cook, stirring constantly, until the eggs are lightly set (about 1 minute). Remove from the heat, stir in the Parmesan, and pour into the baking dishes. Bake for 25 minutes, until set and golden on top. Serve hot or warm from the baking dishes.

Summer Vegetable and Wheat Cocotte

This summer dish is actually inspired from a delicious soup I would devour on the coldest winter days when I got out of school at 5 p.m. as a child in Morocco. I still prefer an early dinner, even though it goes against the French tradition. I reinvented the flavors of my childhood by turning my beloved soup into THE vegetarian and organic dish par excellence—it is a true delight that gets everyone talking.

Times

Active: 40 minutes
Cooking: 1½ hours

Serves 10
—

Ingredients

- 4 large artichokes (or 10 baby purple artichokes)
- 16 sweet, crisp carrots (see Notes for winter vegetable alternatives)
- 3 fennel bulbs
- 8 zucchini
- 4 bunches scallions (or 4 large white onions)
- 6 shallots
- 4 garlic cloves
- 6 tbsp extra-virgin olive oil
- 4 cups (1 liter) My Chicken Broth (see recipe p. 118) or vegetable broth (or water)
- 5½ cups (2 lb./1 kg) einkorn wheat (or wheat berries)
- 14 oz. (400 g) fresh or frozen fava beans (or peas)
- 1¾ oz. (50 g) pesto (optional; see Notes)
- Salt and freshly ground black pepper

To garnish
- Sliced almonds

In a large saucepan of boiling, salted water, cook the artichokes for 15–20 minutes. To test for doneness, carefully pull on a leaf, which should come away easily. If not, cook for an additional 5 minutes. Drain, let cool, and remove all the leaves until only the hearts remain. Scrape out the fuzzy chokes and cut each heart into four or six pieces, depending on their size.

Preheat the oven to 350°F (180°C/Gas mark 4). Wash the carrots, fennel bulbs, and zucchini and cut into ½-in. (1-cm) dice. Chop the scallions and peel and finely chop the shallots. Peel the garlic, removing the germs, and finely chop.

In a large cast-iron Dutch oven or a similar burner-proof pot, fry the scallions, shallots, and garlic in the olive oil over low heat until translucent. Meanwhile, bring the broth to a boil in a saucepan.

Add the einkorn wheat to the scallion mixture and cook for 2 minutes, stirring constantly. Add half the hot broth, cover, and transfer to the oven for 30 minutes.

Remove the pot from the oven and season with salt and pepper. Add most of the remaining broth with the diced vegetables and fava beans, and then stir in the pesto, if using.

Mix well, cover and return to the oven for 15 minutes. Check to see if the grains and vegetables are tender. If not, add a little more broth and return to the oven for an additional 5–10 minutes. Taste and add more salt or pepper as needed. Serve sprinkled with sliced almonds.

Notes

To make your own pesto, *place garlic, basil, Parmesan, and pine nuts in the bowl of a food processor and pulse until very finely chopped. Transfer to a bowl and drizzle in a little olive oil, stirring constantly with a wooden spoon until well combined. Et voilà, your pesto is ready!*

For the winter version of this soup, *use root vegetables such as celery root, beets of all colors, parsnips, and squashes. Replace the pesto with 1¾ oz. (50 g) chopped black truffle pieces, for a touch of luxury.*

Slow-Cooked Summer Tian

In my family, we call this version of a Provençal tian "tomato and zucchini jam." The thyme-scented onions, slowly cooked in olive oil, and the vegetables that caramelize around the edges as they bake make this a truly decadent dish.

Times

Active: 45 minutes
Cooking: 1¾–2 hours

Serves 12
—

Ingredients

- 4½ lb. (2 kg) onions
- ¾ cup (180 ml) extra-virgin olive oil, divided
- Leaves of 6 thyme sprigs (or 1 tsp dried thyme), plus more for sprinkling
- 8 zucchini (7 oz./200 g each) (or a combination of dark and light green zucchini and yellow squash)
- 4½ lb. (2 kg) firm, ripe plum tomatoes, such as Roma or Olivette, similar in diameter to the zucchini and squash
- 2 tsp sugar
- 2 tbsp distilled white vinegar
- Salt and freshly ground pepper

Peel the onions, slice them thinly, and divide between two 10-in. (26-cm) skillets. Add 4 tablespoons of the olive oil and half the thyme to each. Season with salt and pepper, cover, and cook for 20 minutes over medium heat, stirring occasionally, until the onions are softened and beginning to turn golden.

Preheat the oven to 350°F (180°C/Gas mark 4).

Wash and dry the zucchini and tomatoes. Cut the zucchini crosswise into ½-in. (1-cm) slices, discarding the ends. Cut the tomatoes, with their skin on, crosswise into ½-in. (1-cm) slices. You should have equal amounts of zucchini and tomato slices.

Transfer the onions to a large baking dish and use a spatula to spread them evenly over the base. Arrange the zucchini and tomato slices upright in tight-fitting rows over the onions, alternating the colors. Sprinkle over the sugar, salt, pepper, and the remaining thyme, and drizzle with the vinegar and the rest of the olive oil. Bake in the center of the oven for 1½ hours.

If you see the vegetables are scorching a little on top, lower the oven temperature to 300°F (150°C/Gas mark 2) after 1 hour. They should be very tender and caramelized around the edges.

Notes

Serve as a side with leg of lamb, sea bream, another grilled fish or, as I do, as a main dish with quinoa and salad.

Onion Gratin

What a discovery! Garlic and onion are two ingredients in my kitchen that I just cannot live without. But while I'd never thought of making a gratin from garlic bulbs, I also hadn't considered an onion gratin until one came into my life via the Internet. I simplified the idea and made it my own, and here it is—elevated from a mere side to a vegetable dish in its own right. Certainly, onion soup did not need me to make it the classic it is today, but that great French dish owes as much to bread and cheese as it does to the onion. Here, the latter is king.

Times

Active: 30 minutes
Cooking: 20 minutes

Serves 10
—

Ingredients

- 4½ lb. (2 kg) large white onions
- 4 tbsp extra-virgin olive oil
- 3 egg yolks
- ½ cup (1¾ oz./50 g) freshly grated Parmesan
- ¾ cup (200 ml) coconut milk
- 1 pinch grated nutmeg
- Salt and freshly ground pepper

Preheat the oven to 400°F (200°C/Gas mark 6).

Peel and thinly slice the onions. Divide the olive oil between two 10-in. (26-cm) skillets and place over medium-low heat. Add equal quantities of onions to each skillet, season with salt and pepper, and cook for about 20 minutes, stirring occasionally, until the onions are translucent. Remove from the heat.

In a bowl, combine the egg yolks, Parmesan, coconut milk, and nutmeg. Stir in the onions and pour into a gratin dish.

Bake for 20 minutes until golden brown.

Notes

Serve this gratin with white fish, roast chicken, or risotto: I recommend The Perfect Risotto (see recipe p. 140–41).

My "Moussaka-Style" Eggplant Gratin
—

Yes, more eggplants! One of summer's most inspiring and well-traveled vegetables, eggplant is highly prized around the Mediterranean where it is served in so many different ways: fried, grilled, pureed, spiced, blended with tahini until smooth, to name but a few. It is the same in India and Japan, and probably in many other countries, too. When I was a child in Morocco, my mother also prepared eggplants in lots of ways but, to be honest, I wasn't keen on any of them. Only recently, in an attempt to make up for lost time, did I start to appreciate this vegetable. One of my favorite pastimes is to mix eggplant dishes from different places, like a DJ mixes music, and that is how, in my Provençal kitchen, this Turkish-Italian "moussaka"—fat-reduced, I can assure you— was born. On its own, it is the ideal dish to feed twelve or more.

My "Moussaka-Style" Eggplant Gratin

Times

Active: 45 minutes
Cooking: 1½–1¾ hours

Serves 12
—

Ingredients

- Extra-virgin olive oil
- Kosher salt
- 8 firm round Sicilian eggplants (or 12 striped or purple eggplants)
- 2 large onions (about 14 oz./400 g)
- 2 pink garlic cloves
- Leaves of 1 bunch cilantro
- 1 lb. (500 g) fresh or canned tomatoes
- 2 tbsp sunflower oil
- 1 tbsp hot Madras curry powder
- 1 tsp ground turmeric
- 1–2 tsp ground cumin (according to taste)
- 1 tsp ground ginger
- ½ tsp ground cinnamon
- 1 pinch Cayenne pepper (optional)
- 2½ lb. (1.2 kg) lean ground lamb leg or ground beef (or half-lamb and half-beef)
- 1 tbsp sugar
- 2 tbsp white vinegar
- 2 cups (500 ml) strained tomatoes (tomato passata)
- ⅔ cup (2 oz./60 g) freshly grated Parmesan
- Pitted black olives (optional)
- Salt and freshly ground pepper

Preheat the oven to the highest possible temperature on fan setting.

Brush two rimmed baking sheets with olive oil and sprinkle with a little kosher salt.

Wash the eggplants and cut them lengthwise into ½-in. (1-cm) slices. Spread them over the baking sheets and roast for 15 minutes, or until golden.

While the eggplants are roasting, peel and chop the onions. Peel, remove the germs, and chop the garlic. Wash and dry the cilantro. Pulse the onion, garlic, and cilantro together in a food processor until coarsely chopped. Peel the tomatoes (if using fresh) and chop.

In a large skillet, heat the sunflower oil over low heat. Stir in the spices and onion-cilantro mixture and season with salt and pepper. Add the ground meat, increase the heat to medium-high, and break up any lumps with a fork so the spices are evenly distributed and the meat browns evenly. Add the chopped tomatoes, sugar, and vinegar and season with salt. Cook, stirring constantly, for 3–4 minutes. Taste and add extra spices if necessary.

When the eggplant slices are tender and golden, remove them from the oven and lower the temperature to 325°F (170°C/ Gas mark 3). Line the base of one large rectangular baking dish (preferably porcelain and 12 × 16-in. [30 × 40 cm]) with eggplant slices, overlapping them slightly, and cover with one-third of the meat mixture. Repeat the layers twice more, finishing with a layer of eggplant. Cover with the strained tomatoes, sprinkle with the Parmesan, and dot the top with pitted black olives (if using).

Bake in the oven for 1–1¼ hours and it's ready! You can leave the moussaka in the turned-off oven if your friends are running a bit late.

Summer Vegetable Pistou

Out of the top five dishes in my repertoire, this pistou comes in first as it has everything I love: vegetables from my garden in a rainbow of colors, olive oil, garlic, and basil. It's also cooked in a cast-iron pot and eaten with a spoon during my favorite season, summer. I just love the contrast between the hot, cooked vegetables and the cold, uncooked pistou.

Times

Active: 45 minutes
Cooking: 45 minutes
Chilling: 2–3 hours

Serves 10–12
—

Ingredients

For the pistou
- 5½ lb. (2.5 kg) firm, meaty tomatoes
- 6 pink garlic cloves
- 30 basil leaves
- Scant ⅔ cup (150 ml) extra-virgin olive oil
- 1 tbsp fleur de sel
- Freshly ground pepper

For the vegetables
- 4 bunches scallions
- 1½ lb. (700 g) sweet, crisp carrots
- 1½ lb. (700 g) small zucchini
- 8 oz. (250 g) baby potatoes, unpeeled
- 2 large white onions
- 1 lb. (500 g) fresh spinach
- ½ cup (125 ml) extra-virgin olive oil, divided
- 4 tbsp fennel seeds
- Leaves of 4 thyme sprigs
- 6 tbsp water
- 12 oz. (350 g) fresh or frozen peas
- 11 oz. (300 g) shelled fava beans (optional)
- Fleur de sel and freshly ground pepper

To prepare the pistou, peel the tomatoes and remove the seeds. Peel the garlic and remove the germs. Quarter the tomatoes and process in a blender with the garlic, basil, olive oil, fleur de sel, and pepper until smooth. Taste and add more salt, pepper, or olive oil if necessary. Chill in the refrigerator for 2–3 hours.

To prepare the vegetables, peel the scallions and trim the roots and tops, leaving a little of the green. If the scallions are on the large side, cut them in half. Peel the carrots and cut into diagonal ¾-in. (1.5-cm) slices. Wash the zucchini, peel off the skin in alternating strips lengthwise, and slice like the carrots. Scrub the potatoes. If they are small, leave them whole, otherwise, cut them into halves or quarters. Peel and thinly slice the white onions. Wash the spinach and sauté it briefly in a skillet with a little olive oil, salt, and pepper, until wilted. Set aside.

Pour 4 tablespoons of the olive oil into a large cast-iron Dutch oven set over medium heat. Add the scallions, onions, and the fennel seeds and sauté, stirring, until the onions just begin to color. Add the thyme, cover, and reduce the heat to low. Simmer for about 5 minutes, until the onions are translucent.

Add the potatoes, carrots, and water, and season with salt and pepper. Simmer, without stirring, for 15 minutes, until the potatoes are nearly tender (see Notes). Add the zucchini, peas, and fava beans (if using). Add a little more salt and simmer for an additional 10 minutes until the vegetables are al dente. Place the spinach on top.

When ready to serve, transfer the well-chilled pistou to a clear pitcher, if you have one, to display its color or use a sauce boat. Transfer the hot vegetables to a shallow serving dish.

Let your guests serve themselves by pouring a little chilled pistou into soup plates and spooning the hot vegetables on top. Eating with a spoon means the contrasting pistou and vegetables come together to be enjoyed in every mouthful.

Notes

Since cast iron is a perfect heat conductor, your vegetables should be cooked and ready to serve in 30 minutes but the cooking time will depend on the freshness of the vegetables, especially the potatoes and carrots. If your vegetables are not al dente by this time, cook them for a little longer.

Roasted Rainbow Bell Peppers

A lovely light starter with the sweet smell of summer. Variations of this dish of multicolored bell peppers, roasted until tender and then marinated in garlic and olive oil, can be found in Morocco, Provence, and elsewhere around the Mediterranean. For the photograph, I've used just red and green peppers but you can add yellow ones, too, if you can find them. It's the ideal dish for feeding a crowd, as it can be prepared a day ahead.

Times

Active: 30 minutes
Cooking: 20 minutes
Resting time: 2 hours or overnight

Serves 12
—

Ingredients

- 12 large bell peppers (4 red, 4 green, and 4 yellow)
- ⅓ cup (150 ml) extra-virgin olive oil, plus extra for greasing
- 4 large pink garlic cloves
- Juice of 3 lemons (or 3 tbsp distilled white vinegar) (optional)
- Salt and freshly ground pepper

To roast the peppers, preheat the oven to the highest possible temperature on fan setting. (You can also broil them, although I personally prefer roasting as I find the peppers easier to digest.) Brush two rimmed baking sheets with olive oil. Wash and dry the peppers and set them whole on the baking sheets. To roast them, place the peppers in the oven and roast for a good 20 minutes—or longer—until soft, turning them over halfway through the cooking time. They must have a slightly smoky taste and their skin charred.

To broil the peppers, preheat the broiler and broil for about 10 minutes, turning them over halfway through the cooking time (wearing heatproof gloves or using a long-handled fork), until charred.

Transfer the peppers to a strainer in the sink and run cold water over them until cool enough to handle. Peel off the skins, cut in half, remove the stalks and seeds, and slice into strips. Peel the garlic, remove the germs, and finely chop. If you are serving the peppers the same day, arrange the strips on a serving dish, alternating the colors and tucking the garlic between the layers. If serving the next day, refrigerate in a covered dish.

Pour the olive oil over the peppers and season generously with salt and pepper, adding lemon juice or vinegar to taste (if using). Let the peppers rest for 2 hours at room temperature before serving, so the flavors have time to develop. If chilling overnight, allow the peppers to come to room temperature before serving.

Red Bell Peppers with Garlic and Thyme

Do you find bell peppers difficult to digest? I do, too, especially the green ones. If so, try these plump red peppers with their sweet pan juices enhanced with garlic, vinegar, and thyme, and let me know how you get on. The peppers are equally good whether you are cooking for two or for twelve, and all you need is plenty of skillets and burner space. After that, the dish practically cooks itself.

Times

Active: 15 minutes
Cooking: 20 minutes

Serves 12
—

Ingredients

- 3½ lb. (1.5 kg) red bell peppers (about 8)
- 8 pink garlic cloves
- 2 tbsp fresh thyme leaves, plus extra to serve
- 6 tbsp extra-virgin olive oil
- 8 tbsp sherry vinegar
- Fine sea salt and freshly ground pepper

Halve the peppers, remove the seeds, and cut into ¾-in (2-cm) squares. Peel the garlic, remove the germs, and finely chop. Wash and dry the thyme leaves. Place one large skillet (or 2 medium ones) over high heat and, when really hot, add the oil and then the peppers. Stir for 2 minutes, lower the heat, season with salt and pepper, and continue cooking until the peppers are tender but not charred (about 10 minutes).

Add the chopped garlic and thyme leaves and cook for 1 minute. Increase the heat to high, add the vinegar, stir well to thoroughly mix everything, and cook for about 5 minutes.

Eat these fragrant peppers hot or warm, whichever you prefer, adding more salt and vinegar to the skillet, if you wish. Give everything a final stir before transferring to a serving dish, and sprinkle over a little extra thyme.

This hors d'oeuvre is very versatile. It is perfect with aperitifs and equally tasty served with a selection of Lebanese-style meze (such as Tabbouleh, see recipe p. 49, and Smoky Eggplant Caviar, see recipe p. 52).

Curried Summer Squash Farfalle

This pasta dish is a variation on one of my most tried-and-trusted recipes: a spiced zucchini and yellow squash gratin that I've been making for years. I'd always promised myself I'd try the same sauce over pasta, and why not toss in the zucchini and yellow squash, too? That's how yellow and green summer squash now find themselves wearing bow ties at my table.

Times

Active: 15 minutes
Cooking: 20 minutes

Serves 10
—

Ingredients

- 6 small, firm zucchini (preferably light green)
- 6 small, firm yellow summer squash
- Extra-virgin olive oil
- 8 quarts (8 liters) water
- 3 tbsp kosher salt
- Scant 2 lb. (850 g) farfalle
- ¼ tsp saffron threads
- 2 tbsp hot water
- 1 tbsp hot Madras curry powder (if you like spicy food)
- 1⅔ cups (400 ml) heavy cream
- Salt and freshly ground pepper

To garnish
- Roughly chopped cilantro

To serve
- Freshly grated Parmesan
- Salad of well-flavored greens like purslane

Wash the zucchini and yellow squash and cut into thin slices. In one large or two medium skillets, heat a little olive oil over low heat. Add both squashes, season with salt and pepper, increase the heat, and cook for 3 minutes until lightly golden, gently turning them over with two spatulas. Set aside.

In a large pot, heat the 8 quarts (8 liters) water with the kosher salt, and bring to a boil. Stir in the pasta and cook according to the package instructions.

While the pasta is cooking, prepare the sauce. Using the back of a teaspoon, crush the saffron to a powder against the sides of a large microwave-safe bowl, and stir in the 2 tablespoons of hot water to dissolve it. Add the curry powder and cream and season with salt and pepper. Microwave for 1 minute on full power, stir, and set aside.

As soon as the pasta is cooked, call your guests to the table because, like a soufflé, pasta will not wait. Drain the pasta, leaving a little water clinging to it, and tip into a large serving dish. Pour over the sauce and stir until the pasta is coated.

Reheat the squash for 1 minute over high heat and spoon over the pasta. Sprinkle with the cilantro and serve immediately with a bowl of grated Parmesan for the cheese lovers among you.

A fresh salad of purslane or other greens will complete the meal and make for a very happy table.

Fusilli with Pancetta and Onions

Of course, everyone knows fusilli! It's short like penne but with a twist and, when paired with the sauces that suit it, is very content—as you will be. Although we don't always follow it (and I'm the same), we all know the Italian pasta law that decrees that every shape has its own sauce—or sometimes several sauces—with which it is meant to be paired. Bearing in mind, however, that all shapes are happy to be dressed with tomato sauce. I have a soft spot for fusilli, especially when served with onions. This recipe was the specialty of my Italian friend Luciano, who came from Puglia and had an unmistakable accent. He was a true foodie who loved making pasta as much as playing soccer or reading the papers. Trust him, it's great!

Times
Active: 30 minutes
Cooking: 35 minutes

Serves 10
—

Ingredients
- 1½ oz. (40 g) dried porcini mushrooms
- 2 lb. (1 kg) onions
- 7 oz. (200 g) pancetta (or bacon)
- 10 quarts (10 liters) water
- Scant ⅔ cup (5¼ oz./ 150 g) kosher salt
- 2 lb. (1 kg) fusilli
- Scant ⅔ cup (150 ml) extra-virgin olive oil, divided
- 1 cup (250 ml) dry white wine
- Salt and freshly ground pepper

To serve
- 2 tbsp toasted sesame seeds
- 1¼ cups (4¼ oz./120 g) freshly grated Parmesan

Soak the porcini mushrooms in a bowl of warm water for 5 minutes and then drain and chop. Peel and thinly slice the onions. Cut the pancetta (or bacon) into thin strips.

In a large pot, bring the water and salt to a full boil, add the fusilli, and cook according to the package instructions.

At the same time, in a sauté pan large enough to hold all the pasta, heat 5 tablespoons of the olive oil over medium heat. Add the onions and fry, stirring frequently, until softened and golden. Add the wine and porcini, season with salt and pepper, and cover. Simmer over low heat for 15 minutes.

While the onions and mushrooms are simmering, sauté the pancetta in a small skillet in 2 tablespoons of the olive oil for 5 minutes, stirring constantly. Remove from the heat.

Drain the pasta, leaving a little water clinging to it, and add to the skillet with the onions together with the remaining 3 tablespoons of olive oil. Add the pancetta and cook for an additional 2 minutes over low heat, stirring often.

And dinner is served! Sprinkle with the sesame seeds and a good dose of grated Parmesan and remembrance.

Koshari

This recipe is guaranteed to dispel those Sunday evening blues. It is THE iconic Egyptian dish and every family has its own version. Vegan before the movement became trendy, koshari is made just with pulses, boldly seasoned tomato sauce, and crisp fried onions. My version is a firm favorite with my squadron of grandchildren, and adults love it, too. Easy to make, it is filling and nourishing whatever the season, and it suits all ages and any number of guests. I'm betting that koshari will soon be one of your all-time favorites, as it is mine. I add slices of grilled eggplant and/or zucchini, which entails more work but adds so much extra flavor. The choice is yours!

Times
Active: 40 minutes
Cooking: 1½ hours

Serves 10–12
—

Ingredients

For the pulses layer
- Extra-virgin olive oil
- 3 eggplants, preferably Sicilian
- 4 zucchini
- 14 oz. (400 g) canned chickpeas, drained and rinsed
- 1 sweet, crisp carrot
- 1 cup (7 oz./200 g) green lentils
- 3 bay leaves
- 10½ oz. (300 g) macaroni (or short-grain rice, or half and half)

For the tomato sauce
- 3½ lb. (1.5 kg) onions
- 8 pink garlic cloves
- 9 lb. (4 kg) ripe tomatoes
- 1 bunch fresh basil (or cilantro or thyme)
- ½ cup (125 ml) extra-virgin olive oil
- 2 tbsp sugar
- 3 tbsp white vinegar
- 1 pinch Cayenne pepper
- Salt and freshly ground pepper

For the crisp onion rings
- 6 large white onions
- Salt
- Flour, for dredging
- Oil, for deep frying

To assemble
- 1 cup (4½ oz./100 g) freshly grated Parmesan, plus extra to serve

To prepare the pulses layer, preheat the oven to the highest possible temperature on fan setting. Brush two rimmed baking sheets with olive oil.

Wash the eggplants and zucchini. Cut the eggplants into ½-in. (1-cm) rounds and spread over one of the baking sheets. Cut the zucchini lengthwise into ½-in. (1-cm) slices and spread over the other baking sheet. Roast for 10-15 minutes, until golden. If you wish, rub the chickpeas between your hands to remove the skins (this makes them easier to digest). Peel the carrot. Fill a large saucepan with cold water, add the carrot, lentils, and bay leaves, and bring to a boil. Lower the heat and simmer for 20 minutes. Drain and discard the carrot and bay leaves. Meanwhile, cook the macaroni and/or the rice in separate saucepans, and then drain.

To prepare the tomato sauce, peel and thinly slice the onions. Peel the garlic, removing the germs, and thinly slice. Wash, dry, and dice the tomatoes. Wash and dry the basil (or your chosen herb) and finely chop the leaves. Heat the oil in a large pot and cook the onions over high heat, stirring constantly until softened. Add the tomatoes, garlic, sugar, vinegar, and Cayenne pepper, season with salt and pepper, and bring to a boil. Reduce the heat to medium and cook for 30 minutes, stirring occasionally. Stir in the basil, taste, and adjust the seasoning if necessary.

To prepare the onion rings, peel and thinly slice the whole onions crosswise, separating the slices into rings. Boil in a saucepan of salted water for 2 minutes. Drain, pat dry on paper towel, dredge in flour, and then deep fry in hot oil until crisp.

To assemble, preheat the oven to 400°F (200°C/Gas mark 6). Layer the chickpeas, lentils, pasta, and rice (the order doesn't matter) in two clear 8-in. (20-cm) round soufflé dishes, separating the layers with the eggplant, zucchini, and a little tomato sauce. Finish with a thick layer of sauce, sprinkle with the Parmesan, and bake in the oven for 15 minutes or until heated through. Serve hot with any remaining tomato sauce, a bowl of grated Parmesan, and the fried onion rings on the side.

Mafaldine with Chicken, Arugula, and Lemon

Yes, more pasta, but this time I'm shaking things up a bit by swapping shells or spaghetti for mafaldine—a long, flat ribbon pasta with ruffled edges, which I know you are going to love! The recipe makes a complete meal for both adults and children, in all seasons. It has the bright lemony zing the Milanese enjoy in their risotto and pasta dishes—trust them, they know what they're doing!

Times
Active: 20 minutes
Cooking: 20 minutes

Serves 10
—

Ingredients

- 2 lb. (1 kg) cherry tomatoes (different colors, if possible)
- 1 lb. (500 g) arugula (or 1 green lettuce, finely shredded)
- 6 pink garlic cloves
- Juice of 4 lemons
- 4 tbsp Dijon mustard
- 5 boneless, skinless chicken breasts
- Scant ¾ cup (195 ml) extra-virgin olive oil, divided
- 2 tbsp soy sauce
- 8 quarts (8 liters) water
- Scant ½ cup (4¼ oz./ 120 g) kosher salt
- 1¾ lb. (800 g) mafaldine pasta, broken into thirds
- 2 tbsp softened butter
- Salt and freshly ground pepper

To garnish
- 1 generous cup (5¼ oz./150 g) toasted hazelnuts

Wash, dry, and halve the cherry tomatoes. Wash and dry the arugula (or lettuce). Peel the garlic, remove the germs, and crush. **In a small bowl,** whisk together the lemon juice and mustard. Season with salt and pepper.

Cut the chicken into thin strips. Heat 2 tablespoons of the olive oil with the soy sauce in a large skillet over high heat. Add the chicken and sauté for about 4 minutes until cooked through and golden brown, tossing with two spatulas so it cooks evenly. Remove from the skillet and set aside. Wash and dry the skillet.

Pour the water into a large pot, add the kosher salt, and bring to a boil. Add the pasta and cook according to the package instructions. Drain, return to the pot, and dry out over very low heat for 1 minute. Stir in 5 tablespoons of the olive oil and the butter, add the chicken strips, and toss until coated. Remove from the heat.

Set two large skillets over very high heat with 2 tablespoons of olive oil in each. Divide the cherry tomatoes between them and sauté for 1 minute, stirring constantly. Stir in the crushed garlic, season with salt and pepper, and add to the pasta. Toss in the arugula (or shredded lettuce), lemon-mustard mixture, and the remaining olive oil if the pasta seems dry. Taste and add more salt, pepper, or lemon juice as needed.

Divide between two serving dishes, roughly chop the hazelnuts or leave them whole, and scatter them over. Serve immediately.

Cherry Tomato, Garlic, and Basil Penne

I love pasta. It's a foodstuff that makes everyone happy and shouldn't scare anyone off (by that, I mean it won't make you fat), so long as you eat it as the Italians do, as a complete dish rather than a side.

Times
Active: 25 minutes
Cooking: 15 minutes

Serves 12
—

Ingredients

- 1¾ lb. (800 g) cherry tomatoes
- 12 sundried tomato pieces (optional)
- 10 garlic cloves
- 2 bunches basil
- 4 quarts (4 liters) water
- ½ cup (5¼ oz./ 150 g) kosher salt, plus extra for seasoning
- 2½ lb. (1.2 kg) penne
- 1½ cups (350 ml) extra-virgin olive oil
- 1 tbsp sugar
- 1 tsp coarse-ground black pepper
- 2 pinches Cayenne pepper (omit for children)
- 3 tbsp white vinegar
- 3 tbsp (1¾ oz./50 g) butter

To serve (optional)
- Freshly grated Parmesan

Wash, dry, and halve the cherry tomatoes. Thinly slice the sundried tomatoes (if using). Peel the garlic, remove the germs, and crush. Wash and dry the basil, reserve some leaves for garnish, and chop the rest finely.

Pour the water into a large pot, add the salt, and bring to a boil. Add the penne, stir, and cook according to the package instructions.

Meanwhile, heat two large skillets over high heat and pour just under half the olive oil into each, reserving a little for serving. Add a pinch of salt to each, followed by the sugar, coarse-ground pepper, Cayenne pepper (if using), garlic, cherry tomatoes, and sundried tomatoes (if using), dividing everything equally between the skillets. Cook for 1 minute, stirring regularly. The cherry tomatoes should be hot but still hold their shape. Add the vinegar and chopped basil and cook for an additional 30 seconds, still stirring. Remove from the heat.

Drain the pasta, leaving a little water clinging to it, and return it immediately to the pot. Over low heat, stir in the butter and the reserved olive oil, followed immediately by the tomatoes and any pan juices.

Taste for seasoning, add more salt, pepper, Cayenne pepper, basil, or olive oil as necessary, and serve at once. These penne are usually eaten without Parmesan. But if you really must. . . .

Spaghetti Aglio, Olio, e Peperoncino

It doesn't get any simpler than this! Spaghetti tossed with garlic, olive oil, and chili pepper can be eaten anywhere, at any time of the year, and it suits any budget. I owe my thanks to a lady behind the stove at a tiny trattoria in Sicily, who not only introduced me to this dish—still my favorite to this day—but also showed me how to make it. The secret? A generous amount of olive oil and plenty of garlic, which is why I'm tempted to call it "pasta for lovers."

Times

Active: 10 minutes
Cooking: 15 minutes

Serves 10
—

Ingredients

- 2 heads of pink garlic
- 2 small fresh red chili peppers (or 1 pinch Cayenne pepper)
- 10 quarts (10 liters) water
- Scant ⅔ cup (5¼ oz./150 g) kosher salt
- 3 large, firm tomatoes (or 9 Roma tomatoes)
- 25 basil leaves
- 2 lb. (1 kg) spaghetti
- 1⅔ cups (400 ml) extra-virgin olive oil

Separate and peel the garlic cloves, cut them in half lengthwise, remove the germs, and slice thinly. Wash the chili peppers, cut them in half lengthwise, scrape out the seeds, and slice thinly. Pour the water into one or two large pots, add the salt, and bring to a boil.

Peel and cut the tomatoes into small dice. Rinse, dry, and chop the basil. Reserve the tomatoes and basil in separate serving bowls.

As soon as the water is boiling, add the spaghetti, and cook according to the package instructions.

Meanwhile, divide the olive oil between two large skillets and set over low heat. Add the garlic and chili pepper, cover, and cook very gently to infuse the oil with flavor, without letting the garlic color—it should soften but not brown.

Once the spaghetti is cooked, drain, reserving a little of the cooking water. Divide the pasta and reserved water between the skillets and toss to blend. Increase the heat to high, cook for 2 minutes, and toss frequently, alternating between the pans.

Your skillets are ready to go to the table—and your hungry guests will be too. Serve the pasta in shallow bowls with the tomatoes and basil in separate bowls alongside for guests to spoon over their pasta, or not. Purists—like me—will abstain.

Shrimp and Melon with Lime Citronette

The Cavaillon (Charentais) from the south of France isn't the only tasty melon around. Even in Provence—home of the Cavaillon melon and a place that has become my home a little— it's easy to find oval yellow or green melons. The green ones are sweeter, while the yellow ones have crisper flesh. I know both well from Morocco, where we'd have them for dessert. When she lived in Tunisia, my friend Marianne Comolli, who taught me so much, discovered these rugby ball-shaped melons and created this jewel of a summer dish.

Times
Active: 40 minutes
Cooking: 1–2 minutes

Serves 10
—

Ingredients

For the melons
- 2 melons with dark green skin, such as Piel de Sapo (Santa Claus) (or Charentais or cantaloupe)

For the lime citronette
- 1 bunch fresh cilantro
- 24 mint leaves
- Juice of 6–8 limes (according to taste)
- ½ cup (125 ml) extra-virgin olive oil
- Salt and freshly ground pepper

For the shrimp
- 30 green jumbo shrimp (prawns) (about 3 oz./80 g each)
- Olive oil for frying

To serve
- Avocado Puree (see recipe p. 214)

Cut the melons in half, scrape out the seeds, and use a melon baller to scoop out small balls of the flesh. Transfer the balls to a large bowl and chill in the refrigerator. Using a sharp knife, cut the remaining flesh away from the rind and set aside for the citronette.

To prepare the lime citronette, wash and dry the cilantro and mint and chop the leaves. Place in a blender with most of the lime juice, the olive oil, and remaining melon flesh. Season with salt and pepper and process to a puree. Taste for seasoning, adding more of the lime juice if wished, transfer to a bowl, and chill in the refrigerator until serving time.

Prepare the shrimp by removing their heads, if necessary. Rinse the shrimp well, peel (scissors make this job easy, or use your hands), and devein them. Pat dry and season with a little salt. If your shrimp are particularly large, you can butterfly them. The shrimp can be prepared in advance on the same day, but store them, covered, in the refrigerator until ready to cook.

To assemble the dish, right before serving divide the chilled melon balls between individual plates. Lightly brush a skillet with olive oil and sauté the shrimp over high heat for less than 1 minute, until they turn pink. Alternatively, you can steam them for 1 minute. Divide the hot shrimp among the serving plates and generously drizzle with the lime citronette. Serve with Avocado Puree. It pairs so well with the citronette, you'd think they were made for each other.

Fish in a Salt Crust

—

*I'll never forget the first time I watched a waiter
break open a salt-crusted sea bass to release the
steaming fillets inside. The presentation was superb,
but I honestly expected the fish to taste very salty.
How wrong I was, as once the beautifully soft fillets
were on my plate, it only took one bite for me
to start dreaming of trying the technique at home.
I thought it would be impossible, but with a trusted
fishmonger, lots of coarse salt, and an oven, it's
child's play. For many years, I'd set the fish whole
and unscaled on a bed of coarse sea salt and bury it
completely but one day, on the tiny island of Cavallo,
between Corsica and Sardinia, I was surprised when
my salt-crusted sea bass arrived covered in salt
on top but placed directly on the baking dish. The
waiter shared the chef's secret with me, which was to
use a mixture of fine and coarse sea salt. This saves
almost two pounds (one kilo) of salt and ten minutes
cooking time.*

Fish in a Salt Crust

Times

Active: 15 minutes
Cooking: 20–25 minutes
Resting: 10 minutes

Serves 10

—

Ingredients

- Extra-virgin olive oil
- 4½ lb. (2 kg) coarse sea salt, preferably from Guérande, (or use kosher salt)
- 2 lb. (1 kg) fine sea salt
- 2 × 4 lb. (1.8 kg) perfectly fresh sea bass (or 2 × 4½ lb./2 kg gilt-head bream), gutted and rinsed, but not scaled (see Notes)
- A few sprigs of dill, cilantro, or tarragon

To serve
- Extra-virgin olive oil
- Freshly ground pepper
- Charlotte or other variety of waxy potato, crushed with olive oil and parsley using a fork
- Tomato salad lightly dressed in sherry vinegar (if serving gilt-head bream)

Preheat the oven to 400°F (200°C/Gas mark 6).

Brush a rimmed baking sheet (or two baking dishes) on which your fish will fit snugly with olive oil. In a large bowl, combine the coarse and fine sea salts. Pat the fish dry with paper towel, tuck several herb sprigs inside the cavity of each, and set on the prepared baking sheet or dishes. Cover the fish in a thick layer of salt—the thicker the layer, the more tender your fish will be.

Bake for 20–25 minutes. To test for doneness, tap the salt crust with the back of a spoon—it should be firm. Remove the fish from the oven and let rest for 10 minutes before taking it to the table. Meanwhile, set the olive oil and pepper mill on the table and a large bowl for discarding the salt crust. Break the crust open in front of your guests by tapping it with two spoons and lift off the fish in chunks, discarding the salt in the bowl. Remove the skin with a spoon (it should slip off easily), fillet the fish, and divide between serving plates. Invite your guests to add a drizzle of olive oil and grind over fresh pepper; as they do so, tell them to listen out for the sound of crashing waves.

Fork-crushed charlotte potatoes with olive oil and parsley are, for me, the best accompaniment for the fish. Gilt-head bream also calls for a diced tomato salad dressed with a few drops of sherry vinegar.

Don't forget to capture your friends' faces as you break open the crust.

Notes

Before you choose your fish, choose your fishmonger wisely. More than other fish dishes, this one depends entirely on the quality of the fish, which must be very fresh and responsibly sourced.

Honey Caramelized Apricots with Long Pepper

The word "apricot" makes me think of my friend Constance, as this fruit is her passion. Each year, she comes over to enjoy apricot compote for breakfast, and sometimes leaves with a "doggie bag" for the following day. But here, I'm suggesting you serve the fruit as a dessert. I love it in July and August, when plump Bergeron apricots—for me the best variety there is—are in season in France, but if you can't find them, use your personal favorite, preferably one with a good balance of sweet and tart flavors. Quick, easy, fragrant, and so pretty on the plate, all you need to make this dessert for a party of twelve are two large skillets.

Times
Active: 15 minutes
Cooking: 10–15 minutes

Serves 12
—

Ingredients
- 18 large, ripe, but not soft, apricots
- 4 tbsp olive oil
- 3 tbsp lavender honey
- ¼ tsp Madagascan or Tahitian ground vanilla bean
- 1 tbsp Javanese long peppercorns

Wash the apricots and pat them dry. Cut in half and remove the pits. If you wish, reserve twelve pits and, using a nutcracker, crack these open to remove the bitter almond kernels inside. They can be blanched and their thin brown skins removed, before being cooked with the apricots so they add their subtle perfume.
Heat the large skillets over medium heat and add the oil, honey, ground vanilla bean, and bitter almond kernels (if using). Place in the apricot halves, skin side down, and add the whole peppercorns. As soon as the oil and honey start to sizzle, cover the pans, lower the heat, and simmer for 10–15 minutes, depending on the size of the apricots. When you can detect the scent of caramel, take the pans off the heat, as the apricots are ready.
At this point the apricots should not be disturbed. Lift them very carefully out of the pans with a spatula or slotted spoon and transfer to serving dishes, or take the skillets to the table (which I prefer to do) so guests can be served according to their appetite.

Notes
Unlike some fruits, such as pears or bananas, apricots do not continue to fully ripen once they are picked, so I recommend you buy them when they are already ripe. To test if an apricot is ripe, rely on touch, not on color alone. It should feel tender but not soft.

Melon with Saffron and Vanilla

In summer, when melons are ripe and sold for a song, we actually tire of eating them raw. This recipe is a renaissance of sorts, as it's simple, surprising, light, and gorgeous. If you're not a star anise fan, leave it out, and keep in mind that a little saffron goes a long way.

Times

Active: 15 minutes
Cooking: 8 minutes
Chilling: 2 hours

Serves 10

—

Ingredients

- 2 large, ripe Charentais melons (see Notes)
- ¾ cup (200 ml) water
- 6 tbsp agave syrup (or 6 tbsp brown sugar)
- 2 Madagascan or Tahitian vanilla beans, split lengthwise and seeds scraped
- 8 threads best-quality saffron
- 2 whole star anise (optional)

To serve (optional)
- Theo's Meringues (see recipe p. 238)

Cut the melons in half and scrape out the seeds. Peel and cut the flesh into ½-in. (1-cm) slices.

Divide the water, agave syrup, vanilla beans and seeds, saffron, and star anise (if using) between two large sauté pans. Bring to a boil and add the melon slices. Simmer for 4 minutes on each side, carefully remove with a skimmer, and let cool. Arrange attractively in one large or two medium serving dishes. Over high heat, boil to reduce the liquid by half, remove the vanilla beans and star anise, and pour over the melon slices. Let the syrup cool before chilling the melon in the refrigerator for about 2 hours before serving. Serve chilled, with or without Meringues, for a memorable ending to a summer feast.

Notes

If you can't find Charentais melons, use another sweet variety with orange or yellow flesh, such as cantaloupe.

Zach's Chocolate Truffle Cake

Zach is the youngest of my eight grandchildren. With a sweet tooth and impeccable palate, he was destined to have a chocolate cake created in his name, but it took him a long time to decide which cake it should be. Last summer a decision was made—it would be my chocolate truffle cake. If you really want to indulge your guests, serve this cake with Crème Anglaise or Meringues made with the leftover egg whites. Zach has a strong preference for all three at once.

Times

Make a day ahead
Active: 35 minutes
Chilling: 12 hours–overnight

Serves 12
—

Ingredients

- 3 cups (750 ml) well-chilled heavy cream
- 1¼ lb. (600 g) dark chocolate, 70%–75% cacao
- 2 tbsp cold black coffee (or 1 tsp instant coffee dissolved in 2 tbsp boiling water)
- 1 stick plus 5 tbsp (6½ oz./185 g) butter, diced and softened
- 6 egg yolks
- ¾ cup (3½ oz./100 g) confectioners' sugar
- ½ tsp Madagascan or Tahitian ground vanilla bean
- ½ tsp ground cinnamon
- Generous 1 tbsp vanilla sugar

To serve (optional)
- Crème Anglaise (see recipe p. 193)
- Theo's Meringues (see recipe p. 238)

Pour the heavy cream into a large bowl and place in the freezer for 15 minutes to make it easier to whip. Line two loaf pans—one measuring 9 × 5 in. (22 × 12 cm) and the other 10 × 5 in. (26 × 12 cm)—with plastic wrap, leaving enough overhanging to cover the cakes after filling the pans.

Melt the chocolate with the coffee in a saucepan over low heat. Remove from the heat and stir in the butter until smooth.

Place the egg yolks, confectioners' sugar, vanilla powder, and cinnamon in a separate large bowl and, using an electric beater, whisk until frothy. Whisk in the chocolate-butter mixture until smooth and let cool.

Remove the bowl of cream from the freezer and whip on high speed until peaks begin to form. Add the vanilla sugar and continue whipping until the cream holds firm peaks. Using a spatula, fold the whipped cream into the chocolate mixture.

Pour the chocolate mixture into the prepared pans and fold the overhanging plastic wrap over the top. Chill in the refrigerator for 12 hours or overnight.

When ready to serve, turn the cakes out onto serving plates and cut into slices. Serve the truffle cake on its own or with Crème Anglaise and/or Meringues.

Raspberry Clafoutis

When it comes to prep time, taste, and sheer enjoyment, this clafoutis comes out top every time. Try it and you'll see what I mean—from the looks on the faces of those you're sharing it with to the murmurs of pleasure it evokes. Satisfaction is guaranteed!

Times

Active: 20 minutes
Cooking: 50 minutes

Serves 10
—

Ingredients

- 2 eggs
- 4 egg yolks
- Scant 1 cup (6 oz./180 g) superfine sugar, divided
- 2 tbsp all-purpose flour
- 1⅔ cups (400 ml) heavy cream
- 1½ lb. (700 g) fresh raspberries (see Notes)

Preheat the oven to 325°F (160°C/Gas mark 3). In a large mixing bowl, lightly whisk the eggs with the egg yolks and ¾ cup (5 oz./140 g) of the sugar, taking care not to let the mixture become thick and foamy. Sift in the flour, add the cream, and whisk until combined. Spread out the raspberries in a single layer across the base of a ceramic baking dish measuring approximately 10 × 12 in. (25 × 30 cm) and sprinkle with the remaining sugar.

Slowly pour the batter over the raspberries, so as not to disturb them.

Bake for 50 minutes or until the clafoutis is puffed, lightly golden on top, and a knife inserted into the center comes out clean. Watch it carefully as the batter must not boil in the oven. If you notice any bubbling, lower the temperature to 300°F (150°C/Gas mark 2).

Remove the clafoutis from the oven and let cool. Serve at room temperature, but beware: one mouthful and you will be hooked!

Notes

You can make the clafoutis all year round using the same quantity of frozen raspberries as fresh. Since you are going to bake them, there's no need to thaw the raspberries first. Simply spread them out in the baking dish as soon as you turn the oven on and sprinkle them with the remaining sugar after making the batter. Prepare the batter, pour it over the raspberries, and bake as indicated above.

Apricot Compote with Lavender Honey

This simple dessert is quick, light, and fragrant. It is one to make with friends, as you can prepare huge batches of the compote and freeze them in airtight containers of different sizes (according to the number of people you are feeding). Wouldn't it be the height of chic to serve this sunny compote for breakfast or dessert in December?

Times
Active: 25 minutes
Cooking: 25 minutes

Serves 12
—

Ingredients
- 40 large, fully ripe apricots
- 4 tbsp lavender honey (or any other honey, except mountain honey, which is too strong for the delicate flavor of the apricots)
- 2 Madagascan or Tahitian vanilla beans, split lengthwise and seeds scraped
- 4 drops of bitter almond extract

Wash the apricots and pat them dry. Cut in half and reserve twelve large pits. Break the pits open with a nutcracker and remove the bitter almond kernels. Blanch the kernels to remove their thin brown skins, leaving just the milky-white almonds.
Cut the apricot halves into two or four pieces depending on their size (like the segments of an orange) and place in a large pot.
Add the honey, vanilla beans and scraped-out seeds, and bitter almond extract.
Place the pot over medium heat, stir, and cover with a lid. Bring to a boil, lower the heat, and simmer for about 15 minutes if your apricots are very ripe. If they are not very ripe, simmer for an extra 5–10 minutes. Juice will have run out of the apricots so, if there is too much, stir with a spatula, increase the heat, and let boil uncovered for a few minutes. That's it, the compote is ready!
All you have left to do is wait for the compote to cool a little before transferring it to an attractive serving dish. You can then sprinkle over some of the white kernels you lovingly prepared.
Serve the compote in pretty bowls, accompanied by warm Perfect Madeleines (see recipe p. 237), and you'll have a dessert that is fit for a king!

Strawberry, Ginger, and Honey Compote

This ginger-spiced compote is perfect during strawberry season and will be a real treat for your family and friends, especially if you can get sweet, local berries. As with the apricot compote, I also like to make this in large batches and freeze some for the winter, when root vegetables are more plentiful than fresh fruit. As we all know, soft fruits always taste better when they are locally grown and in season as, not only will they have been picked when fully ripe, they will also be sweeter and smell fragrant, unlike those that have flown thousands of miles to reach our stores, leaving a huge carbon footprint and cruelly lacking in taste. The next time strawberry season comes around, make the most of it by eating and preparing as many as you want, both raw or cooked.

Times

Active: 20 minutes
Cooking: 10 minutes
Chilling: 2 hours

Serves 10
—

Ingredients

- 4½ lb. (2 kg) strawberries, ideally Gariguette (see Notes)
- 4¼ oz. (120 g) fresh ginger
- 4 tbsp floral or another honey

To serve
- 3½ oz. (100 g) shelled pistachios (or toasted, sliced almonds)

Wash, dry, and hull the strawberries. Peel and finely grate the ginger. Place both in a large pot with the honey and bring to a boil. Reduce the heat to low, cover, and simmer for 2 minutes.

Remove from the heat and partially uncover. Let cool slightly, pour into a fruit bowl, and, when cold, chill for 2 hours or until serving.

I like to scatter roughly chopped pistachios over the strawberries as their vibrant green color contrasts beautifully with the ruby red berries. Toasted, sliced almonds also work very well.

Notes

If Gariguette strawberries are not available, use the sweetest variety you can find.

Berry Almond Crisp

Keen cooks everywhere can't wait for summer and the arrival of all those luscious soft fruits. The best way to enjoy ripe, sun-kissed berries, such as Mara des Bois strawberries, is to eat them freshly picked. Each bite is a revelation, as it is with raspberries, blueberries, currants, and cherries. If you have a particularly big stock, with a handful of at least three different fruits left over the following day, try this relative of a classic crumble—probably my favorite dessert. I love the contrast of the sweet, crunchy topping with the tartness of the fruit, with neither one overpowering the other. In short, perfect harmony!

Times

Active: 30 minutes
Cooking: 40 minutes

Serves 12
—

Ingredients

- 1 lb. (500 g) strawberries
- 14 oz. (400 g) red currants
- 1½ lb. (700 g) raspberries
- Generous 1 cup (8 oz./230 g) superfine sugar, divided
- 2¾ cups (12 oz./350 g) all-purpose flour
- 1 tsp ground cinnamon
- 2 sticks (9 oz./250 g) salted butter, diced and softened, plus more for greasing
- Generous 1 cup (3½ oz./100 g) sliced almonds

Preheat the oven to 400°F (200°C/Gas mark 6) and grease two 9½-in. (24-cm) round porcelain baking dishes with melted butter. Wash and dry all the fruit, and then hull the strawberries and pull the red currants off their stalks.

Put the berries and currants in a large bowl, sprinkle with a scant ½ cup (3 oz./80 g) of the sugar, and stir to combine. Divide the fruit between the baking dishes, spreading it in a single layer.

In a separate large bowl, combine the flour, cinnamon, remaining sugar, diced butter, and ground almonds. Rub the ingredients lightly together with your fingertips until coarse crumbs form.

Scatter a layer of the crumb mixture over the fruit in the baking dishes and bake for 40 minutes, until the topping is golden and crisp. Serve warm.

Léon's Meringue Birthday Cake

Times

Active: 45 minutes
Cooking: 30–35 minutes

Serves 8

—

Ingredients

- Oil for greasing
- 1 cup (250 ml) heavy cream
- 4 egg whites
- 1¼ cups (9 oz./250 g) superfine sugar
- 1 tsp white vinegar
- 1½ cups (5¼ oz./150 g) ground hazelnuts (or ground almonds)
- 1 tbsp confectioners' sugar
- 12 oz. (350 g) fresh raspberries

Preheat the oven to 325°F (160°C/Gas mark 3). Grease two 9½-in. (24-cm) shallow cake pans with oil and line the base and sides of each with parchment paper. If you're using silicone pans, as I'd recommend, you don't need to grease them, just rinse the pans under cold water and shake off the excess rather than drying them.

Pour the cream into a large bowl and place it in the freezer for at least 15 minutes—the colder the cream, the easier it is to whip.

Whisk the egg whites with an electric beater until they hold soft peaks. Whisk in the superfine sugar, a little at a time, and keep whisking until the meringue is stiff and shiny. Add the vinegar (which will prevent the whites collapsing) and whisk briefly to incorporate.

Carefully fold in the ground nuts using a wooden spatula, working from the bottom of the bowl toward the top until fully incorporated into the whites.

Spoon half the meringue into each cake pan and, using a spatula and circular motion, spread evenly, smoothing the tops level.

Bake for 30−35 minutes until the meringues are dry and very lightly golden. Let cool for 10 minutes in the pans and then turn out onto a cooling rack to let cool completely. Remove the cream from the freezer, add the confectioners' sugar, and whisk with the electric beater until thick (in case of splatters, I'd recommend wearing an apron).

Place one disk of meringue on a serving plate and, using a spatula, spread half the cream over it. Carefully lift the second meringue on top and spread the remaining cream over the top (and down the sides if you wish). Wash and dry the raspberries and arrange them upside down in concentric circles so they completely cover the top. Chill the cake in the refrigerator until you are ready to serve it.

Notes

This cake is best made during peak raspberry season but you can also make it in winter using frozen raspberries. Rather than topping the meringue with whole raspberries, serve it with a sauceboat of raspberry coulis, which will be delicious, although slightly less spectacular. Don't use whole frozen raspberries for decoration as they will go soft and their juice will leak out as they defrost.

To make a coulis, blend 10½ oz. (300 g) thawed frozen raspberries with 2 tablespoons of superfine sugar and a few drops of lemon juice or balsamic vinegar. Push through a fine-mesh sieve set over a bowl, if you prefer to remove the seeds. If serving in this way, dust the meringue with confectioners' sugar. Then add candles. Happy birthday to my grandson Léon!

fall / winter

Harira

In Morocco, this traditional soup is eaten every evening to break the fast during the thirty days of Ramadan. In this recipe, I've used celery as well as the usual dried pulses and tomatoes. In my family, we often have this warming soup in winter when I make it using a mixture of fresh vegetables and pulses. Everyone loves it, including the children—and even my cat.

Times

Active: 30 minutes
Cooking: 1 hour 30 minutes

Serves 12
—

Ingredients

- 2 large or 3 medium sweet, crisp carrots
- 2 zucchini
- 2 fennel bulbs
- 2 large onions
- 4 celery stalks with leaves
- 1 bunch cilantro
- 1 tbsp butter (or 3 tbsp olive oil or peanut oil)
- 1 tbsp ground turmeric
- 1 tsp ground ginger
- ½ tsp ground cinnamon
- 4½ lb. (2 kg) canned tomatoes (or frozen diced tomatoes, defrosted)
- 2 tbsp sugar
- 1 tbsp white vinegar
- 4 cups (1 liter) water
- 5 tbsp tomato paste
- 1 generous cup (7 oz./200 g) canned chickpeas, drained
- Juice of 3 lemons
- 3½ oz. (100 g) vermicelli noodles
- Salt and freshly ground pepper

Peel the carrots and zucchini, remove the tough outer layers from the fennel bulbs, and cut all three into small dice. Peel and chop the onions, wash the celery, and cut it into ½-in. (1-cm) slices. Wash and dry the cilantro and chop the leaves finely.

In a large pot, heat the butter or oil over low heat, add the onions and spices, and cook for 5 minutes, stirring occasionally until the onions are softened. Stir in the tomatoes, sugar, vinegar, and half the cilantro and cook for 5 minutes. Add the water, bring to a boil, and simmer for 30 minutes.

Transfer the contents of the pot to a blender and blend until smooth. Pour back into the pot, and if the soup is too thick, add a little extra water. Season with salt and pepper, if necessary. Bring to a boil, stir in the diced vegetables, tomato paste, and chickpeas, and simmer for 45 minutes. When ready to serve, bring the soup to a boil, add the lemon juice, vermicelli, and remaining cilantro, and cook until the vermicelli is done. Taste for seasoning, adding more lemon juice or spices as needed.

Notes

If you prepare this soup the day before, it will taste even better. It has a lot to recommend it, as not only is it delicious, it's filling and isn't expensive to make. Any leftover soup can be frozen.

My Chicken Broth

Nothing could be easier to make than this broth and I love the understated yet rich flavor it adds to everything. It's my favorite flavor enhancer and it's good for you, too. I often use it as a base for soups, risottos, and vegetable dishes, and I even serve it on its own with a handful of alphabet pasta, as it's the best way in winter to warm the soul while you wait for the arrival of spring. I always prepare a big batch of the broth and freeze it in portions for 2–4 people. Here is my secret.

Times

Cooking: 1–1½ hours

Makes 3 quarts (3 liters)
—

Ingredients

- 4½ lb. (2 kg) chicken wings
- 3 quarts (3 liters) cold water
- 1 tbsp ground turmeric
- 2 garlic cloves, unpeeled
- Salt and freshly ground white pepper

Rinse the chicken wings and place them in a large pot. Add the water, turmeric, and garlic, and season with salt and pepper. Bring to a boil and then reduce the heat to very low and maintain a very gentle simmer for 1–1½ hours, until the chicken is fall-off-the-bones tender. Carefully pour the broth into a fine strainer set over another pot or a large bowl. When the wings are cool enough to handle, separate the meat, and discard the skin and bones (see Notes).

Apart from the oysters, this wing meat is the best part of a chicken. At our house, we call it chicken caviar and my grandchildren have fought over this delicacy since they were little. It's how I managed to trump chicken nuggets!

Notes

If you enjoy this broth, do as I do and make it in large quantities to freeze. I suggest using 6½ lb. (3 kg) chicken wings and 5 quarts (4.5 liters) water (in other words, 6½ cups/1.5 liters water per 2¼ lb./1 kg chicken) and store the broth and meat separately in the freezer. If, like me, you have a cat, be sure to close the kitchen door when preparing your chicken caviar—but don't forget to leave a little in the cat's bowl.

Pho (Traditional Vietnamese Soup)

—

In Hanoi, I took a cooking class with the delightful and very talented Aï, a finalist a few years ago in Vietnam's MasterChef. We went to the market together and she introduced me to her suppliers— all lovely, hard-working young women (where were the men, I wondered). Street vendors sell this traditional Vietnamese soup called pho (pronounced "fuh") all day long, including for breakfast, and it's typically accompanied by a small bowl of spicy sauce, the exact recipe for which is a closely guarded Vietnamese secret. As with any national dish, there are as many variations of pho as there are families. My preference is for one made with a light broth that is not a complete meal but makes a welcome starter when the temperature outside dips below 50°F (10°C). As a main dish, pho is equally magical, since the bowls filled with noodles, fragrant broth, and colorful vegetables seem to dance across the table, as though they were in a ballet. It's a ritual akin to serving couscous in North Africa or Peking duck in China.

Pho

Times

Active: 50 minutes
Cooking: 1 hour 15 minutes
for the broth, plus extra time
for cooking the chicken, meat,
or seafood

Serves 12
—

Ingredients

For the Vietnamese broth
- 1–2 sweet, crisp carrots
- ½ cucumber
- 7 oz. (200 g) button or wood ear (cloud ear) mushrooms
- 2 celery stalks
- 5 oz. (150 g) soybean sprouts
- 2 shallots
- 4 lemongrass stalks
- 1½ oz. (40 g) fresh ginger
- 1 bunch cilantro (or Thai basil)
- 1 quantity My Chicken Broth (see recipe p. 118) (or 1 bouillon cube dissolved in 2 cups/500 ml water)
- 1 pinch Cayenne pepper
- 4 tbsp Vietnamese fish sauce (nuoc mam), plus extra for serving
- 4 tbsp soy sauce, plus extra for serving
- Juice of 3–4 limes, to taste

For the pho
- 4 lb. (1.8 kg) chicken, meat, pork, or seafood (about 5 oz./150 g per person)
- 14 oz. (400 g) vermicelli rice noodles, soaked in boiling hot water until tender, and drained
- 1 bunch scallions (or chives), thinly sliced

To prepare the broth, peel the carrots and cucumber, and cut into small dice or coarsely grate. Wash and thinly slice the mushrooms and celery. Wash the soybean sprouts under cold water and drain. Peel and finely chop the shallots, quarter the lemongrass stalks, and peel and grate the ginger. Wash and dry the cilantro or Thai basil and finely chop half the leaves, reserving the rest for garnish. In a large pot, bring the broth to a boil and add the vegetables, herbs, and remaining ingredients except the lime juice. Boil steadily for 5 minutes, then reduce the heat to low, and stir in most of the lime juice. Taste and adjust the seasoning, adding more fish sauce, soy sauce, or lime juice as needed. Keep hot.

The pho can be made using chicken, meat, or seafood. Either add to the broth at the last minute to just cook through, or serve raw in bowls at the table for guests to add to the hot broth (see assembly instructions below). If serving raw, you must ensure they are sliced very thinly, and the broth is piping hot.

For chicken pho, the tender chicken caviar left over from My Chicken Broth is an excellent option. Stir into the broth before serving to heat through. Otherwise, use raw chicken breast meat cut into very thin slices. **Meat pho** is generally made with beef. Use sirloin or rump steak and slice it very thinly across the grain of the meat. Very thinly sliced pork shoulder can also be used.

For seafood pho, use one or a combination of the following: peeled medium green shrimp, a few thin calamari rings, very thin slices of a firm white fish such as monkfish.

To assemble the pho, if you have already cooked the chicken, meat, or seafood in the broth, divide the vermicelli rice noodles among serving bowls and spoon the broth over. If you are serving them raw, place the thin slices in bowls on the table alongside a bowl of rice noodles, and invite guests to help themselves, starting with the noodles. Immediately pour the fragrant, piping hot broth over the chicken, meat, or seafood to ensure they are thoroughly cooked. Sprinkle with the scallions and remaining cilantro, and enjoy.

Notes
If you have a round table, set out the different bowls on a revolving "Lazy Susan"—the perfect way to serve a dish like this.

Festive Chestnut Velouté with Porcini

With three contrasting yet complementary flavors and textures, this velouté is both elegant and luxurious. Quick and easy to prepare, it makes an ideal starter for a Christmas dinner. Happy Holidays!

Times
Active: 40 minutes
Cooking: 5 minutes

Serves 12
—

Ingredients
- 1¼ lb. (600 g) small fresh or frozen porcini mushrooms (or button mushrooms)
- 2 celery hearts
- 20 toasted hazelnuts
- 4 cups (1 liter) My Chicken Broth (see recipe p. 118) (or 1 chicken bouillon cube dissolved in 4 cups/1 liter water)
- 3 lb. (1.3 kg) canned or frozen unsweetened chestnut puree (or vacuum-packed cooked whole chestnuts)
- 3 tbsp (1¾ oz./50 g) lightly salted butter
- 3 tbsp extra-virgin olive oil
- Salt and freshly ground pepper

If you are using fresh mushrooms, cut the base off the stems and quickly rinse the mushrooms under cold water, brushing gently to remove any dirt. Pat dry, slice, and place on paper towel. If your mushrooms are frozen, follow the thawing instructions on the package, then slice.

Wash the celery hearts, pat dry, and cut the stalks into thin slices. Place in an attractive bowl ready to take to the table. Chop the leaves and reserve as a garnish.

Roughly chop the hazelnuts. When scattered over the soup, they must retain their crunch.

In a large saucepan, bring the broth to a boil, and then working in batches, blend the chestnut puree or whole chestnuts with the hot broth, the butter, and seasoning until velvety smooth. If the soup is too thick for you, gradually add more broth or hot water to obtain the texture you prefer.

In a large 10-in. (26-cm) skillet, heat the olive oil over high heat until it is shimmering but not smoking. Add the mushrooms and sauté for 5 minutes, turning them over constantly with two spatulas. Remove from the heat and season with salt and pepper.

If necessary, reheat the velouté over very low heat, stirring with a whisk. Serve in bowls garnished with the mushrooms, celery leaves, and chopped hazelnuts. Pass around the celery slices.

My Watercress Velouté

This vibrant green velouté is full of flavor, simple to make, and irresistible, but if you don't have a blender, the recipe is not for you, I'm afraid. I send my thanks to Adeline Grattard, who created this velvety perfection, as "my" velouté is really hers. The only downside is it does not reheat well, so you must puree and serve the soup immediately (see Notes). If only home appliance designers would make a blender as quiet as a modern dishwasher.

Times

Active: 15 minutes
Cooking: 20 minutes

Serves 10
—

Ingredients

- 5 bunches watercress
- 1 tbsp white vinegar
- 14 oz. (400 g) floury potatoes
- 3⅓ cups (800 ml) water
- 1 tsp kosher salt
- 3 tbsp (1¾ oz./50 g) salted butter, diced and at room temperature

Wash the watercress in a bowl of lukewarm water with the vinegar added. Drain, remove the stems, and roughly chop the leaves.

Peel the potatoes and cut them into even-sized pieces. Place in a large saucepan, add the water and salt, and bring to a boil. Reduce the heat, cover, and simmer until the potatoes are tender.

When the potatoes are cooked, add the watercress, and boil for 1 minute. Remove from the heat and drain.

Transfer immediately to a blender, add the butter, and puree until smooth. Taste for salt and that's it—all done! Serve immediately. This is health and happiness in a bowl, with iron to boost your energy levels.

Notes

Rather than serve the velouté in a soup tureen, do as I do and pour it directly from the blender into individual white bowls to accentuate its vibrant green hue. The velouté cannot wait but if you must serve it at table, transfer it to a clear heatproof carafe. Its color reminds me of Queen Elizabeth II's hats.

Nine Vegetable Shortcut Couscous

—

It's not easy to roll couscous by hand when the movements are not bred into your genes or if you haven't watched your mother and grandmother, up since dawn, moistening the grains and rubbing them between their hands, as I have. Afterwards, they would steam the couscous three times, separating and fluffing the grains—and all in time for lunch. But never fear, there is a much faster way to satisfy a couscous craving, so you can serve it to a host of friends, and here it is. All you need is one large heatproof china or glass bowl (or two of a decent size) and a microwave. This is progress at its best!

Nine Vegetable Shortcut Couscous

Times

Active: 50 minutes
Cooking: 25–30 minutes
Resting: 15 minutes

Serves 12

—

Ingredients

- 8 cups (2 liters) vegetable broth
- 2 tsp ground turmeric, divided
- 2 lb. (1 kg) medium-grain durum wheat couscous
- ½ tsp white pepper
- 2 heaping tbsp sugar
- 1 tbsp salt
- 4 tbsp neutral oil
- 10 sweet, crisp carrots
- 2 lb. (1 kg) pumpkin (or butternut squash)
- 6 Golden Ball turnips (or another sweet variety)
- 1 small bulb celery root
- 1 sweet potato
- 2 fennel bulbs
- 1 small head white cabbage
- 2 large onions
- 1 bunch fresh cilantro
- 10 small, firm zucchini
- 1 stick (4 oz./120 g) salted butter, diced
- Salt and freshly ground pepper

To serve
- 2 lb. (1 kg) canned chickpeas, drained and rinsed
- 5 cups (1¼ lb./600 g) frozen fava, lima, or broad beans, defrosted
- Golden raisins and/or Zante currants
- Toasted blanched almonds
- Ground cinnamon

Pour the vegetable broth into a large pot, add 1½ teaspoons of the turmeric, season with salt and pepper, and bring to a boil. Meanwhile, in a large microwave-safe bowl, combine the couscous, remaining turmeric, white pepper, sugar, and 1 tablespoon of salt. Stir to combine with a large fork and then stir in the oil.

To prepare the vegetables, peel the carrots, pumpkin, turnips, celery root, and sweet potato. Remove the tough outer layers from the fennel and cabbage, and peel the onions. Wash and dry the cilantro. Cut the carrots, zucchini, and sweet potato into 2-in. (5-cm) chunks and the pumpkin, celery root, and cabbage each into six pieces. Cut the fennel and turnips in half. Add all the vegetables and the cilantro to the pot of hot broth, return to a boil, lower the heat, cover, and simmer for 15–20 minutes until the vegetables are just tender. Drain the vegetables with a slotted spoon and keep them warm. Using a ladle, transfer enough hot broth to the bowl of couscous to just cover the grains, but do not stir. Set aside the rest of the broth.

Cover the bowl of couscous with a dish towel and let rest for 15 minutes until the broth has been absorbed. Scatter the butter over the top and gently incorporate it using a large fork, or you could also use your fingers, as my mother did. Lift and aerate the couscous as you go, taking care not to crush the grains. It should double in volume (hence the large bowl). Pour two ladles of broth over the couscous and microwave on high for 5 minutes. Fluff with the fork and return to the microwave for an additional 5 minutes on full power. Fluff once more and it's ready!

To serve, heat the chickpeas and beans in a saucepan with 3 tablespoons of the broth. Serve the couscous in its bowl with the vegetables on a serving platter. Taste the broth in the pot and season with salt and pepper if necessary. Transfer to a soup tureen for drizzling. Spoon the chickpeas and beans into a bowl and place on the table with bowls of raisins and almonds to add sweetness and crunch. Pass the ground cinnamon around for those who'd like a sprinkle.

Lentils with Spinach and Ginger

Once you've tried this recipe from the homeland of Gandhi, you'll want to make it again and again. Like an old pair of jeans that's flattering and not too tight, it seamlessly combines comfort with allure. India has a strong vegetarian tradition and lentils are a staple food, found in countless guises around the country. This flavor-packed version is light, healthy, and easy to make.

Times

Make a day ahead
Active: 30 minutes
Cooking: 40 minutes

Serves 12
—

Ingredients

- 2 cups (14 oz./400 g) green lentils
- 1 whole onion
- 2 cloves
- 1 carrot
- 2 bay leaves
- 4-in. (10-cm) piece fresh ginger (about 3½ oz./100 g)
- 1 bunch cilantro
- 2 shallots
- 4 tbsp peanut oil
- 14 oz. (400 g) frozen spinach, whole leaf or chopped, (or 3⅓ lb./1.5 kg fresh spinach)
- 1 pinch Cayenne pepper
- Cooked quinoa (optional)
- Juice of 3 lemons
- 1⅔ cups (400 ml) coconut milk
- Salt and freshly ground pepper
To serve (optional; see Notes)
- Your favorite soup or salad

Pick over the lentils and rinse them under cold water. Peel and stick the onion with the cloves. Wash and peel the carrot. Place the onion, carrot, and bay leaves in a large pot, add the lentils, cover with cold, unsalted water, and bring to a boil. Lower the heat, cover, and simmer for 20 minutes, or until the lentils are tender—they may need an additional 5 minutes or so. Remove the onion, bay leaves, and carrot, season with salt, stir, and then drain.

Peel and grate the ginger and wash and dry the cilantro. Reserve some of the cilantro leaves for garnish and finely chop the remainder. Peel and thinly slice the shallots. If you are using frozen spinach, heat the oil in a large skillet over low heat, add the spinach (still frozen) and shallots, cover, and cook for 10 minutes, until thawed. If you are using fresh spinach, wash and dry the leaves. Divide the oil between two skillets set over high heat and sauté the spinach until wilted. Add the shallots and cook for 3–4 minutes, stirring constantly. Stir the ginger, cilantro, and Cayenne pepper into the spinach, add the lentils, and toss gently with two spatulas to combine. If you want to add a little cooked quinoa (see Notes), stir it in now, and then taste for salt and pepper. Stir in the lemon juice and coconut milk and garnish with the cilantro leaves. Serve hot.

Notes

These lentils make a good accompaniment to fish or white meat, but they also deserve to be served on their own, as a starter or a vegetarian main combined with a little cooked quinoa. Add a soup or salad, and you've got a complete meal.

Deviled Red Lentils

For those of you who like spicy dishes, this recipe is for you. Yes, the ingredients list is long, but trust me, these lentils are well worth stocking up your spice cabinet. Neither a dhal, nor a soup, this is a satisfying one-dish meal that is also healthy and sure to please. If you prefer green lentils, they work, too, but they aren't as pretty. Basmati rice and popadams make traditional Indian accompaniments.

Times

Active: 1 hour
Soaking: 30 minutes
Cooking: 45 minutes

Serves 10
—

Ingredients

- 2½ cups (1 lb./500 g) red lentils
- Scant 3 cups (700 ml) cold water
- 1 large bunch cilantro
- 1 onion (about 7 oz./200 g)
- 2½ oz. (70 g) fresh ginger
- 5 garlic cloves
- 1 tsp mustard seeds (optional)
- 1 tbsp neutral oil
- 1 tsp ground coriander
- 2 tbsp ground cumin
- 1 tbsp ground turmeric
- 1 tsp sweet paprika
- 1 tbsp curry powder
- ½ tsp red pepper flakes
- 1¼ lb. (600 g) strained tomatoes (tomato passata)
- 2 tbsp sugar
- 1 cucumber
- Scant 1½ cups (10½ oz./300 g) plain yogurt, preferably Greek-style, divided
- Drizzle of extra-virgin olive oil
- 5 tbsp (3 oz./80 g) butter, diced
- Juice of 5 limes
- ¾ cup (200 ml) coconut milk (optional)
- Salt

Rinse the lentils three times under cold running water, and then soak them in the 3 cups (700 ml) water for 30 minutes.

Meanwhile, wash and dry the cilantro and pick the leaves. Peel and chop the onion and ginger. Peel the garlic and remove the germs. Pulse the onion, ginger, garlic, and half the cilantro together in a food processor until finely chopped but not reduced to a paste. Finely chop the remaining cilantro leaves and set aside.

Set a large Dutch oven or sauté pan over medium heat, add the mustard seeds, and toast for 3 minutes, until fragrant but not burned. Reduce the heat to low, add the neutral oil and onion mixture, and cook for 10 minutes. Add the coriander, cumin, turmeric, paprika, curry powder, and red pepper flakes and cook for 5 minutes, stirring constantly.

Add the lentils with their soaking water, the strained tomatoes, and sugar. Bring to a boil, then reduce the heat to low. Cover and cook for 20–30 minutes, until the lentils are tender (the cooking time will depend on the quality of the lentils you've used).

While the lentils are cooking, prepare a raita. Wash and finely dice the cucumber and place in a bowl with a scant 1 cup (7 oz./200 g) of the yogurt. Add a drizzle of olive oil and stir to combine.

When the lentils are cooked, stir in the butter until melted, the remaining scant ½ cup (3½ oz./100 g) yogurt, the lime juice, and the remaining cilantro, reserving a little for garnish. Season with a little salt, taste, and adjust the seasoning as necessary. If the lentil mixture is too thick for your liking, add the coconut milk (or extra yogurt, if you prefer). Sprinkle with the reserved cilantro.

Rice

—

I must have been Asian in another life as, if I listened to my innermost cravings, I would eat rice every day. I love every type of rice, whatever its color, its country of origin, or its method of preparation.

Recently, when I was dining in a restaurant in Tokyo that had been recommended by a friend who is a food connoisseur, I learned that in Japan, rice—the most sacred of foods—is traditionally eaten on its own at the end of a meal. Nothing could have made me happier. The chef came out to serve the rice himself and there was a hotplate on a small rectangular table to keep it warm in its green earthenware dish. After showing us the pearly white grains, which had an iridescent glow to rival the most beautiful pearls I have ever seen, the chef held out to each of us a bowl containing a few spoonfuls of the rice—which I am not even going to attempt to describe. Afterwards, there was silence as the taste etched itself in my memory forever. I have no idea how that delicately perfumed rice was prepared. It was a kind of timeless miracle.

Here, I propose three recipes based on different varieties of white rice, all with radically different flavors. They are recipes I can make with my eyes closed, whether I'm cooking for two or for thirty.

Persian Basmati Rice

This long-grain rice originates from India or Pakistan; the name "basmati" comes from Hindi and means "the queen of fragrance." My personal preference is for Iranian basmati, as it is elegant, with long, fine grains, and is so full of flavor when prepared in this way. You can also use Indian basmati, which is easier to find.

Times

Active: 15 minutes
Cooking: 25 minutes
Resting: 25 minutes

Serves 10

Ingredients

- 7 tbsp (3½ oz./100 g) salted butter, divided
- 2 tbsp extra-virgin olive oil
- 5½ cups (10½ oz./300 g) chopped onions (about 2 onions)
- 2¾ cups (1 lb./500 g) best-quality basmati rice (see Notes)
- 1 pinch saffron threads soaked in 2 tbsp hot water
- 4 cups (1 liter) My Chicken Broth (see recipe p. 118) (or 2 chicken bouillon cubes dissolved in 4 cups/1 liter water)
- 3 tbsp Zante currants
- 4 tbsp barberries (optional)
- 1 handful fresh herbs of your choice, finely chopped (optional; see Notes)

In an extra large skillet, heat 2 tablespoons of the butter with the olive oil over medium heat. Stir in the onions and cook until translucent. Add the rice, toss with two spatulas until coated in the butter and oil, and cook for 5 minutes, stirring constantly. Add the saffron and its soaking water and pour in enough chicken broth to barely cover the rice. Bring to a boil, reduce the heat to very low, cover the skillet, and set your timer for 11 minutes.

Remove the rice from the heat and sprinkle with the currants and barberries (if using). Do not stir but cover with a dish towel, replace the lid, and let rest for 20 minutes, to allow the rice grains to continue to swell.

Add the remaining butter and herbs (if using). Fluff the rice by raking it very gently with a large fork and serve right away.

Notes

In Iran, where rice is almost a religion, an extra stage is added to the preparation. Before cooking, the rice is washed in several changes of cold water to remove excess starch from the grains and prevent them sticking together. The rice must then be left in a strainer to dry for 1 hour before cooking. This extra step is optional when making this recipe, but it is essential for rice dishes slow-baked in the oven (see Klima Indra recipe p. 164–65).

If, like me, you love herbs, pick your favorite ones and chop them finely, using the fork to mix them into the rice at the same time as the butter.

Standing Rice

The name alone is unforgettable. And once you've tried this rice, you won't be able to live without it. I learned how to cook rice this way from my friend Marianne Comolli and I'm delighted to share it with you. The technique results in perfectly separated grains that "stand" on their own, hence the recipe's evocative name, which is of Creole origin.

Times

Active: 12 minutes
Draining: 15 minutes–several hours
Cooking: 30 minutes

Serves 10
—

Ingredients

- 8 quarts (8 liters) water
- 2 tbsp kosher salt
- 4½ cups (2 lb./900 g) short-grain rice (not risotto rice)
- 7 tbsp (3½ oz./100 g) salted butter

You can cook the rice several hours in advance, and finish it on the stovetop or in the oven (see Notes) at serving time.

Pour the water into a large pot, add the salt, and bring to a boil. Stir in the rice and boil, uncovered, for 12 minutes, taking care not to let the water boil over. Drain the rice in one large or two medium strainers and rinse under cold running water until completely cool. Let drain for at least 15 minutes or for several hours in the refrigerator.

At serving time, melt the butter in a large heavy pot over low heat and add the rice. Spread in an even layer, completely covering the base. Cover and cook for 15–20 minutes so that wonderfully fragrant steam can escape from the surface of the rice. Gently fluff the rice with a fork as you transfer it to a shallow serving dish.

Serve at once or keep warm in the pot for a few minutes.

Notes

To finish the rice in the oven, preheat the oven to 300°F (150°C/ Gas mark 2) and generously grease a baking dish or Dutch oven with butter. Spread the rice in an even layer and cover tightly with aluminum foil or a lid. Place in the oven for 25 minutes. With delicate hazelnut notes, this rice is excellent served with all kinds of dishes, including grilled meats, vegetables, curries, or anything with a sauce.

The Perfect Risotto

Please don't turn the page. Set aside your fear of making risotto and stop worrying about it needing too much attention, about whether it will be over- or undercooked, or if you have enough time. Buy some top-quality risotto rice and take the plunge, as you'll be rewarded, gratified, thanked, and want to do it again. The secret to perfect risotto? Invite your friends into the kitchen to help you by taking turns with stirring, as they'll appreciate the flavor and ingenuity of this quintessentially Italian rice dish even more.

Times

Active: 10 minutes
Cooking: 25 minutes

Serves 10
—

Ingredients

- 3 quarts (3 liters) My Chicken Broth (see recipe p. 118) or vegetable broth
- 1¾ sticks (7 oz./200 g) butter, at room temperature, diced, divided
- 1½ cups (4½ oz./125 g) freshly grated Parmesan
- 2 egg yolks
- 10½ oz. (300 g) very thinly sliced onions (about 2 onions)
- 3½ cups (1½ lb./700 g) top-quality risotto rice, preferably Carnaroli
- 1⅔ cups (400 ml) white wine (or leftover champagne)
- Extra-virgin olive oil
- Salt and freshly ground pepper

Begin by warming soup bowls for serving. Heat the broth in a large pot and keep it at a gentle simmer as you cook the risotto.
In a large bowl, using a fork or an electric beater, beat half the butter until smooth. Add the Parmesan and egg yolks and beat again until creamy.
In a Dutch oven, melt the remaining butter over medium heat, add the onions, and season with pepper. Cook for 5 minutes, stirring frequently, until softened but not browned. Add the rice and stir with two spatulas to thoroughly coat the grains. Pour in the white wine, increase the heat to high, and keep stirring until the wine evaporates.
Gradually add the hot broth, a ladleful at a time, stirring constantly yet gently with a spatula until nearly all of the liquid is absorbed, before adding more. Continue to repeat this process until the rice is al dente (allow about 20 minutes).
Remove from the heat and quickly stir in the creamed butter, Parmesan, and egg yolks. Add a drizzle of olive oil, season with salt, and add a little more broth, if necessary—the risotto needs to be *all'onda*, that is to say, wonderfully creamy, but neither too liquid nor too dry. Season generously with pepper.
Serve in the warmed bowls, either plain or with the garnish of your choice, with or without my Onion Gratin. Dig in with spoons.

To serve (see Notes)
- Fresh porcini mushrooms sautéed in olive oil, grated truffle, a handful of arugula, or chopped fresh herbs
- Onion Gratin (optional) (see recipe p. 66)

Notes

This beautifully creamy risotto is excellent served plain, but in the fall it's divine topped with porcini mushrooms sautéed in olive oil, or some freshly grated truffle. I also love it with a good handful of chopped herbs and greens such as arugula, basil, parsley, tarragon, spinach, or—even better—sorrel, when it's in season. And just recently, I discovered my favorite way to serve it: accompanied by my Onion Gratin. Give it a try, it's amazing!

Sparkling Beets

My big discovery last fall was that beets can be chic!
Cutting them into large "fries," rather than slicing them into
rounds, and arranging them in a dome shape in one large or
two stylish salad bowls changes everything. The two contrasting
shades of red rival a jeweler's gemstone and the flavor is equally
sophisticated. I've even converted my husband who, after
unhappy childhood memories, used to refuse to eat beets.
With red currants or pomegranate seeds and a few sprigs
of chervil or chives, the beets come alive and are as stunning
to look at as they are to eat.

Times
Active: 25 minutes

Serves 12
—

Ingredients

- 6 cooked beets, preferably
  the long Crapaudine variety
  (or the most flavorful beets you
  can find)
- Leaves of 12 chervil sprigs
  (or chive stems)
- 10½ oz. (300 g) red currants
  (or pomegranate seeds)
- 4 tbsp raspberry vinegar
- 3 tbsp white vinegar
- 4 tbsp extra-virgin olive oil
- Salt and freshly ground pepper
  (gray pepper, if available)

Wearing gloves so you don't stain your hands, peel the beets,
cut each one into eight equal slices from top to bottom, and then
cut each slice into approximately ½-in. (1-cm) sticks. Arrange
them in a dome shape in an attractive salad bowl.

Wash and dry the chervil or chives and chop finely. Wash, dry,
and de-stem the red currants.

In a small bowl, whisk together the vinegars and season with
salt. Pour over the beets, followed by the olive oil, and add a few
grinds of pepper. Scatter the red currants or pomegranate seeds
over the beets and sprinkle with the chervil or chives.

Now tell me what you think of my take on children's building
blocks for the chef!

Za'atar-Roasted Butternut Squash

If this recipe reminds you of Yotam Ottolenghi, you're spot on. This Israeli-born chef, who now lives in London, is my idol and I know I'm not alone, particularly since the publication of his cookbook Jerusalem, cowritten with his Palestinian friend and head chef, Sami Tamimi. Ottolenghi is a genius at elevating the flavor of even the most ordinary vegetables, through the abundant use of herbs and spices. I love his approach but, to suit my taste, I often cut back on the spice—but not the herbs— and roast vegetables at a lower temperature. Perhaps you'll adapt this recipe to suit your taste, too. This way of cooking squash makes a welcome change from the traditional pumpkin pie or soup made for Halloween or Thanksgiving.

Times

Active: 30 minutes
Cooking: 1 hour

Serves 10

—

Ingredients

- 6 tbsp extra-virgin olive oil, plus extra for greasing
- 2 large or 3 medium butternut squashes
- 4 red onions
- 3½ oz. (100 g) plump dried apricots
- Juice of 2 lemons
- 3 tbsp za'atar herb and spice mix (or dried oregano)
- 1¼ cups (300 ml) water
- Salt and freshly ground pepper

Preheat the oven to 400°F (200°C/Gas mark 6). Brush a rimmed baking sheet with olive oil.

Peel, seed, and cut the butternut squash into ¾-in. (2-cm) slices. Peel and cut the onions into thick slices from top to bottom. Place the squash, onions, and apricots on the baking sheet, drizzle with the olive oil and lemon juice, sprinkle with the za'atar, and season with salt and pepper. Toss everything together with your hands until well coated. Add the water and roast for 30 minutes.

After 30 minutes, give the vegetables a good stir using two large spoons. Add more water, if necessary, and return to the oven for an additional 30 minutes until the onion and squash are tender and caramelized around the edges. A decidedly different take on festive squash!

Garlic and Thyme Carrot Confit

Slowly cooked in olive oil, these carrots are exquisite, especially if you love caramelized notes as much as I do. In this recipe, the sweet caramelized flavor is imbued with hints of garlic and thyme that evoke Provence. Although nothing like a dessert, these carrots are just as much of a treat.

Times

Active: 40 minutes
Cooking: 30 minutes

Serves 12
—

Ingredients

- 5½ lb. (2.5 kg) sweet, crisp carrots
- 36 pink garlic cloves (5–6 heads)
- 1¼ cups (300 ml) extra-virgin olive oil
- ¾ cup (200 ml) water
- 2 tbsp thyme leaves (from about 6 sprigs)
- Salt and freshly ground pepper

Peel the carrots and cut them diagonally into ¼-in. (0.5 cm) slices. Peel and halve the garlic cloves and remove the germs. **Heat the olive oil** over medium heat in a large Dutch oven or two 9½-in. (24-cm) sauté pans. Add the carrots and garlic and sauté, stirring, until lightly browned. Reduce the heat to low, gradually stir in the water, cover, and cook for 15 minutes. Uncover the pan, stir in the thyme, season with salt and pepper, and increase the heat to high. Cook for 10 minutes, stirring with two spatulas, until the carrots are beautifully tender on the inside and crisp and golden on the outside.

Notes

These carrots are superb with roast chicken.
For rosemary-scented carrots, replace the thyme with the finely chopped leaves from a 4-in. (10-cm) sprig of rosemary. The flavor will be quite different, as will be the health benefits.

Potato and Parsley Gratin

This gratin was invented by a painter friend, Michel Warren, who we lost all too early. He was multitalented, an exceptional human being, and his culinary creativity was unparalleled. He generously shared some of his recipes for those in the know in a slim volume with an inspired title, L'Antisteak. It's now nearly impossible to get your hands on a copy, although you can occasionally find a secondhand one online. If you're lucky enough to spot a copy, grab it at any price.

Times

Active: 30 minutes
Cooking: 1½ hours

Serves 10
—

Ingredients

- 7 tbsp (3½ oz./100 g) salted butter, diced, plus extra for greasing
- 4½ lb. (2 kg) waxy potatoes, such as Charlotte
- 2 bunches flat-leaf parsley
- 8 shallots
- 1⅔ cups (400 ml) heavy cream
- Salt and a generous amount of freshly ground good black pepper

To serve (optional)
- A green salad (see Notes)

Preheat the oven to 325°F (170°C/Gas mark 3) and grease two 8-in. (20-cm) deep soufflé dishes with butter.

Peel the potatoes and slice them crosswise into very thin rounds. Place in a strainer, run very hot water over the potato slices, and then dry with a dish towel. Wash and dry the parsley and chop the leaves finely. Peel and roughly chop the shallots.

Place a single layer of potato slices in the base of each soufflé dish—the layer should be thin, but don't worry about making a pretty pattern. Sprinkle generously with shallots, parsley, salt, and pepper.

Repeat the layers until you've filled the soufflé dishes. Season once more with salt and pepper and dot with the butter. Pour the cream over the top and cover with parchment paper. Bake for 1½ hours.

Take the soufflé dishes to the table and serve at once with a simple green salad, if you wish. To serve, use a large spoon that will reach all the way to the bottom of the gratin, so guests can enjoy all the layers.

Notes

Whatever you serve it with—meat, poultry, or fish—this gratin is all your guests will remember after the meal is over. A simple green salad, such as arugula lightly dressed with extra-virgin olive oil and fleur de sel, is the only accompaniment needed.

Snowy Celery Root

Experienced skiers describe their ideal snow as "pure white and powdery." I am not a skier, but I do have the same penchant for white and a passion for celery root. If you're also a fan of this winter root vegetable, you'll swoon over this light, airy puree.

Times
Active: 35 minutes
Cooking: 35–40 minutes

Serves 12
—

Ingredients
- 5½ lb. (2.5 kg) celery root (about 3 medium bulbs)
- 2 cups (500 ml) heavy cream
- 6 tbsp fruity extra-virgin olive oil
- Salt

Peel the celery root and cut into 1-in. (2.5-cm) cubes. You can cook the celery root in one of two ways: either steam it for 35 minutes or add it to a saucepan of boiling water and cook for 30 minutes. Whichever method you choose, the cooked celery root must be very tender so it is easy to puree.

Drain the celery root and, using a food processor or food mill fitted with an extra-fine disk (see Notes), puree until smooth. Gradually blend in the cream until perfectly smooth and very white. Drizzle in the olive oil, still blending, until well combined.

Transfer the puree to a saucepan, cover, and reheat over very low heat, stirring occasionally. Season with salt. Serve at once.

Notes
It's best to use a food mill to make this puree, after which blend it with the olive oil and cream.

Snowy celery root pairs well with all roast poultry and fish such as salmon or my Fish in a Salt Crust (see recipe p. 94). It is also divine with warm foie gras or as a bed for scallops lightly seared with soy sauce and maple syrup.

Leeks with Spinach Vinaigrette

Adding a sauce transforms any dish! It's not that I don't enjoy the French bistro classic of leeks in mustard vinaigrette, but if you dress this rather ordinary vegetable with an unexpected variation on traditional vinaigrette, it elevates it to another level. Even better, it adds an element of surprise, so give it a go!

Times
Active: 30 minutes
Cooking: 20–30 minutes

Serves 10
—

Ingredients

- 25 leeks (the thinnest you can find)

For the spinach vinaigrette
- 7 oz. (200 g) frozen chopped spinach, thawed
- Generous ½ cup (1 oz./30 g) flat-leaf parsley, finely chopped
- Scant ½ cup (100 ml) sherry vinegar
- Scant ½ cup (100 ml) balsamic vinegar
- ⅔ cup (150 ml) extra-virgin olive oil
- 2 tbsp walnut oil
- Fleur de sel and freshly ground pepper

Heat salted water in a large saucepan, bring to a boil.
Meanwhile, prepare the leeks by cutting off the roots and green tops so the white parts are all roughly the same length. If the leeks are thick, split them in half lengthwise, and thoroughly wash to remove any dirt or grit between the layers. Cook the leeks in the boiling salted water for 15 minutes, or steam them for 25 minutes, until tender. Drain thoroughly.

Prepare the spinach vinaigrette by draining the spinach thoroughly and pressing between two plates to remove any excess water. Place it in a large bowl and add the parsley, vinegars, and oils. Season with fleur de sel and pepper and stir with a fork until well combined.

Right before serving, pile the leeks on a serving platter and spoon over some of the vinaigrette, serving the rest in a bowl on the side. It is important to be generous with the vinaigrette—as you'll very quickly realize.

"Celeritto":
Celery Root "Risotto"

If you like celery root and risotto, you'll go crazy for this recipe, which I've dubbed "celeritto." It's the perfect dish to surprise your family and friends when they sit down to eat, and if you're someone who is short on time, celeritto will become your go-to favorite. In France, for far too long celery root has been inseparable from remoulade—but not anymore! Celery root is finally free to flirt with risotto, dress up in truffles if it chooses, and I promise there's not a single grain of rice in sight!

Times

Active: 30 minutes
Cooking: 15 minutes

Serves 10
—

Ingredients

- 3 bulbs celery root (2 lb./900 g peeled weight)
- 4 tbsp (2 oz./60 g) salted butter, divided
- 2 egg yolks
- ¾ cup (2¾ oz./80 g) freshly grated Parmesan
- ¾ cup (200 ml) heavy cream
- 6 small or 4 large shallots
- 2 tbsp olive oil
- 2 vegetable or chicken bouillon cubes
- ¾ cup (200 ml) leftover champagne (or dry white wine)
- 1 oz. (30 g) black truffle (optional)
- 10 flat-leaf parsley sprigs (or 1 handful arugula)
- A few coarsely chopped roasted hazelnuts

Peel and cut the celery root into thick slices and then into thick strips. Grate on the large holes of a box grater to obtain rice-like "grains." Bring a large saucepan of salted water to a boil and toss in the celery root "rice." Reduce the heat to a simmer, cook for 3 minutes, and drain.

While the celery root is cooking, soften half the butter and beat it with the egg yolks, Parmesan, and cream until combined. Peel and finely chop the shallots.

In a large skillet or sauté pan, fry the shallots in the olive oil and remaining butter over medium heat until translucent. Crumble in the bouillon cubes, pour in the champagne or wine and increase the heat. Bubble until the wine has evaporated, stirring constantly, lower the heat, and add the celery root. Cook for 2 minutes, stirring all the time.

Add the butter and egg mixture (and grate in the truffle, if using). Toss everything together until evenly combined.

Wash, dry, and roughly chop the parsley or arugula. Remove the pan from the heat and stir in the herbs.

A few coarsely chopped roasted hazelnuts make a welcome addition. Serve at once.

Herby Potato Salad

This refreshing, herb-packed potato salad is a far cry from the ice-cold mayonnaise-drenched offerings typical in cafeterias and delis. Try it tonight with your family or friends and you won't be disappointed. If there are only four or five of you, you can halve the ingredients and the active time. Be sure to use firm-fleshed, waxy potatoes, and don't skimp on the herbs.

Times

Active: 45 minutes
Cooking: 20–30 minutes
Resting: 2 hours

Serves 10
—

Ingredients

- 4½ lb. (2 kg) firm-fleshed waxy potatoes, such as Yukon Gold, Charlotte, or Roseval
- 8 pink shallots
- ¾ cup (180 ml) extra-virgin olive oil, divided
- 25 small cornichons in vinegar, drained
- 4 dill pickles
- 1 bunch flat-leaf parsley
- 5 tarragon sprigs
- 1 bunch chervil
- 12 dill sprigs
- ½ cup (125 ml) red wine vinegar
- Salt and freshly ground pepper

Wash the potatoes with their skins on and place in a large pot. Cover with cold water and bring to a boil. Reduce the heat to low, cover, and simmer for 20–25 minutes, until the potatoes are tender.

While the potatoes are cooking, peel and thinly slice the shallots, place in a bowl, and pour in enough of the olive oil to cover. Slice the cornichons and dill pickles into thin rounds. Wash, dry, and roughly chop the herbs, reserving some chervil for garnish.

Drain the potatoes and run cold water over them until they are just cool enough to handle. Peel off the skins while the potatoes are still warm, cut into ¾-in. (1.5-cm) slices or chunks, and divide between two salad bowls. Add the shallots and olive oil, cornichons, dill pickles, herbs, and remaining olive oil. Season with salt and pepper, add the vinegar, and gently stir to combine. The salad should be generously dressed, so add more olive oil and vinegar if it seems dry.

Let rest for 2 hours at room temperature to give the flavors time to develop—for this reason, it is important not to chill the salad. When ready to serve, give the salad a final stir, sprinkle over the reserved chervil, and take it to the table.

Soy Sautéed Shiitakes

Originally from Japan, fresh shiitake mushrooms are now widely available in many Western supermarkets, but it's important to know how to cook them so as to draw out their full flavor and retain their unique texture. Here, I sauté them with nothing more than sunflower oil and soy sauce and, occasionally, I toss in some shallots. The mushrooms are tasty, light, and quick and easy to prepare. So good, in fact, that I serve them on their own as a starter rather than as a side.

Times

Active: 20 minutes
Cooking: 15 minutes

Serves 12
—

Ingredients

- 2 lb. (1 kg) fresh shiitake mushrooms
- 6 tbsp sunflower oil
- 6 tbsp soy sauce

Quickly rinse the shiitake mushrooms to remove any grit and then cut off the rubbery stems. If the mushrooms are small, leave them whole, otherwise break them apart with your hands into two or three pieces.

Heat two large skillets over high heat and add 3 tablespoons of the oil to each. Add the mushrooms and cook for 2 minutes, tossing constantly with two spatulas. Reduce the heat as low as you can, cover, and cook for 10 minutes.

Uncover the pans, increase the heat to high, drizzle in the soy sauce, and cook for 1 minute, stirring briskly. The mushrooms are ready, so serve immediately!

Notes

These soy-sautéed shiitake mushrooms are also excellent combined with a few finely chopped shallots. Fry the shallots in sunflower oil over low heat until translucent. Increase the heat to medium and sauté until the shallots are lightly golden brown, before adding the mushrooms and continuing with the recipe.

Spoon-Tender Lamb

Like many, my go-to dish for years was seven-hour leg of lamb, as you knew everybody loved it. However, one day my butcher didn't have any leg of lamb, so I tried cooking two whole lamb shoulders in the same way. The result was even better and that is how my spoon-tender lamb shoulder recipe was born. The two shoulders, cooked in the oven for 4½ hours (rather than 7 hours for leg), are perfect for ten people and are even more succulent than the slow-roasted Moroccan lamb mechoui of my childhood. Unforgettable!

Times

Active: 30 minutes
Cooking: 5 hours

Serves 10
—

Ingredients

- 3½ lb. (1.5 kg) sweet, crisp carrots
- 30 frozen pearl onions (or 5 bunches scallions)
- 2 tbsp butter
- 7 garlic cloves, unpeeled
- 1 bouquet garni (3 bay leaves, 3 thyme sprigs, and 6 parsley sprigs tied together with kitchen twine)
- 1 small can or ½ tube tomato paste
- 2 whole bone-in lamb shoulders, 3½–4 lb. (1.6–1.8 kg) each, trimmed by your butcher
- Generous 1 tbsp kosher salt
- 1 chicken bouillon cube
- 1 cup (250 ml) hot water
- Freshly ground pepper

To serve
- Mashed potatoes, macaroni, or rice

Preheat the oven to 300°F (150°C/Gas mark 2). Peel the carrots and cut them into 1¼-in. (3-cm) slices. If using scallions, trim off the green parts.

In a 12-in. (30-cm) cast-iron Dutch oven, melt the butter over medium heat. Add the carrots, onions (or scallions), garlic, bouquet garni, and tomato paste and cook for 4–5 minutes, stirring regularly. Add the lamb, season with the kosher salt and a generous amount of freshly ground pepper.

Dissolve the bouillon cube in the hot water and pour into the pot. Bring to a boil, cover, and transfer to the oven. Fill a pan with water and set it on the rack above the lamb, making sure you top up the water during the cooking time, as necessary. After 2 hours, wearing a thick pair of oven mitts, check the lamb to see that all the liquid in the pot hasn't evaporated. If it has, add a little hot water from the pan above it and use this as an opportunity to turn the lamb over so the meat soaks up the cooking juices evenly. After 4½ hours, check the meat pulls away easily from the bones. If it doesn't, return it to the oven for a maximum of 30 minutes. When the lamb is ready, carefully remove and discard the bones so that only the tender golden-brown meat and slow-braised vegetables remain.

Lift the meat out of the pot with a skimmer and place it on a serving platter. Surround the meat with the vegetables, but don't panic if you can't find any onions as they will have melted into the sauce, adding all their flavor and making it wonderfully rich and syrupy. Transfer the sauce to a gravy boat and serve the lamb with mashed potatoes, macaroni, or rice. This meltingly tender lamb should be eaten with a spoon.

Notes

Don't panic if you can't find your onions in the pan, they will have cooked down, mellowing the now syrupy sauce, which you should serve in a gravy boat. Follow this full-flavored main dish— the ultimate comfort meal—with a green salad and round it off with a fruit compote.

Klima Indra

—

Unlike other Indian-inspired recipes in this book,
this one is for non-vegetarians. It reminds me
of Moroccan cuisine because of the spices used,
and I make it often as it's so popular with my guests.
It looks elegant in the pot taken straight from
the oven to the table—a bit less so on the plate,
I'm afraid—and it is absolutely delicious to eat.
I love the ceremony of serving it accompanied
by an array of chutneys.

Klima Indra

Times

Active: 30 minutes
Drying: 1–2 hours
Cooking: 2 hours 30 minutes
Resting: 20 minutes

Serves 12

Ingredients

- 4½ cups (1¾ lb./800 g) basmati rice
- 2 large onions
- 2 garlic cloves
- 1 bunch cilantro
- 1 stick plus 2 tbsp (5¼ oz./150 g) butter
- 1 tbsp ground ginger
- 2 tbsp ground cumin
- 1 tsp ground cinnamon
- 2½ lb. (1.2 kg) ground lamb from the leg
- 3 pinches saffron threads
- 3 tbsp hot water
- 6½ cups (1.5 liters) My Chicken Broth (see recipe p. 118) (or 3 chicken bouillon cubes dissolved in 6½ cups/1.5 liters water)
- Salt and freshly ground pepper

To serve

- Chutneys of your choice (see Notes)
- 3 cups (1½ lb./750 g) plain yogurt

To remove excess starch from the rice, place it in a large bowl and cover with cold water. Gently swish the grains around, drain, and repeat this process four or five times, until the water is clear. Transfer the rice to a strainer and let dry completely (allow 1–2 hours).

Peel and chop the onions. Peel the garlic, remove the germs, and chop. Wash and dry the cilantro and chop the leaves finely.

To clarify the butter, melt in a saucepan over high heat and bring to a boil. Reduce the heat and simmer for 5 minutes, until most of the foam is gone. Slowly pour the clear yellow liquid into a separate container, leaving the milky residue behind. You now have clarified butter—or ghee, as it's known in India—with the milk solids and impurities removed.

Heat 3 tablespoons of the clarified butter over medium heat in a 12-in. (30-cm) skillet, until shimmering but not smoking. Add the onion, garlic, ginger, cumin, and cinnamon and sauté for 5 minutes, before crumbling in the ground lamb. Increase the heat to high and fry for 4 minutes, stirring constantly and breaking up any lumps of meat with a fork to distribute the spices evenly. Remove from the heat and stir in the cilantro. Taste and adjust the seasoning, adding more salt, pepper, and spices as desired. Mix well with a fork to combine.

In another large skillet, heat the remaining clarified butter over medium heat. Add the rice and sauté for 5 minutes, stirring to coat the grains thoroughly.

Preheat the oven to 350°F (180°C/Gas mark 4). In a bowl, soak the saffron threads in the hot water. In a large pot, bring the chicken broth to a boil. Stir in the saffron and its soaking liquid and keep hot.

Spread one-third of the rice across the base of a 12-in. (30-cm) Dutch oven and cover with one-third of the lamb mixture. Repeat the layers ending with the rice. The rice layers will be very thin but don't worry, as the grains will swell up during cooking.

Gently pour the hot broth down the sides of the Dutch oven until the liquid just covers the rice. If you don't have enough broth, add boiling water.

Cover the pot with a sheet of parchment paper, then put the lid on, ensuring it is tightly sealed. Set a pan filled with water in the base of the oven. As the water in the pan evaporates the perfect cooking conditions for the rice will be created.

Place the pot in the oven and bake for 30 minutes. Lower the temperature to 250°F (120°C/Gas mark ½) and continue cooking for 2 hours, without opening the oven or lifting the lid off the pot. Remove the pot from the oven and let rest for 20 minutes with the lid still on. Take off the lid and serve right away, with the chutneys and yogurt on the side.

Notes

Serve with Banana Chutney (see recipe p. 168), and/or Mango Chutney (see recipe p. 166), along with the plain yogurt.
This complete meal in one pot takes a long time to cook, but it is quick to prepare—and even quicker to eat. It's a winner!

Mango Chutney

In my mind, dishes like Klima Indra (see recipe p. 164–65) and Indian-style curries are incomplete without a selection of chutneys to serve alongside them. This mango chutney is so good that your guests are likely to eat it straight with a spoon, so allow for generous helpings. It means buying a lot of mangoes, but it's worth the splurge—or perhaps you could plant a tree in your garden. Tricky in Normandy, but if you live in California, it shouldn't be a problem! Otherwise, there's always frozen mango picked at its prime. If you buy your mangoes fresh, make sure they feel heavy and are very ripe. They're easy to find, but if they've flown a long way by plane, they're not so environmentally friendly. Here is the recipe—I'll let you decide.

Times
Active: 40 minutes
Cooking 30 minutes

Serves 12 (if serving a selection of 2 or 3 chutneys)
—

Ingredients
- 2 lb. (1 kg) peeled and pitted mango flesh (about 4 large mangoes)
- 2 limes
- 2½ oz. (70 g) fresh ginger
- 1¼ cups (300 ml) white vinegar
- 1½ cups (10½ oz./300 g) sugar
- 1 pinch chili powder

Peel the mangoes and cut the flesh into ½-in. (1-cm) cubes. Wash and dry the limes and place them whole in the bowl of a food processor. Pulse until finely chopped but not reduced to a paste. Peel and finely grate the ginger.

Place the chopped limes and all their juice in a saucepan with the other ingredients. Cook over low heat for 30 minutes, stirring often with a spatula, until thick. Remove from the heat and let cool.

Serve at room temperature.

Notes
This chutney is not just delicious served with curries, but also with grilled chicken. If you have any left over (highly unlikely!), it will keep for months in a sealed jar in the refrigerator.

Facing page, from top to bottom:
Red Onion and Cassis Chutney (p. 169),
Banana Chutney (p. 168),
and Mango Chutney.

Banana Chutney

Times

Active: 30 minutes
Cooking: 20 minutes

Serves 12 (if serving a selection of 2 or 3 chutneys)
—

Ingredients

- 2 lemons
- 11 oz. (300 g) pearl onions
- 2 oz. (60 g) fresh ginger
- 6 bananas, ripe but firm
- 3 tbsp peanut oil
- ½ cup (2½ oz./70 g) Zante currants
- 2 tbsp brown sugar
- ½ tsp ground cinnamon
- ½ tsp freshly grated nutmeg
- Salt and freshly ground pepper

Wash and dry the lemons, finely grate the zest, and squeeze the juice. Peel and thinly slice the onions and peel and finely grate the ginger. Peel the bananas and cut them into ½-in. (1-cm) dice.
Heat the oil in a large sauté pan over low heat. Add the onions and cook for about 5 minutes, tossing with two spatulas, until softened and beginning to color. Add the currants and cook for 2 minutes, stirring constantly. Stir in the lemon zest and juice, sugar, ginger, and spices, and season with salt and pepper. Still stirring, cook for an additional 2 minutes. Add the bananas and cook for about 10 minutes, stirring frequently, until softened. Remove from the heat and let cool.
Serve at room temperature.

Notes

This chutney can be served with any spicy dish. Like the Mango Chutney (see recipe p. 166), it also keeps well for months in a sealed jar in the refrigerator.

Red Onion and Cassis Chutney

Times

Active: 20 minutes
Cooking: 30 minutes

**Serves 12 (if serving a
selection of 2 or 3 chutneys)**
—

Ingredients

- 2 lb. (1 kg) red onions
- 3 tbsp peanut oil
- 4 tbsp sugar
- 5 tbsp red wine vinegar
- 3 tbsp crème de cassis liqueur
- 1¼ cups (300 ml) red wine
- ½ tsp ground cinnamon
- 2 whole cloves
- Salt and freshly ground pepper

Peel and thinly slice the onions. In a Dutch oven, heat the oil over low heat, add the onions, and cook for 2 minutes, tossing with two spatulas. Add the sugar and let caramelize for 2 minutes, stirring constantly. Pour in the vinegar and let evaporate. Add the crème de cassis, red wine, cinnamon, and cloves, and season with salt and pepper. Cook over low heat for about 20 minutes, stirring often, until the liquid has reduced and the chutney is thick. Remove from the heat and let cool. **Serve** at room temperature.

Notes

This chutney is excellent served with fish or grilled chicken, and, of course, Klima Indra (see recipe p. 164–65).
If you want to have some left over to store in the refrigerator for another meal, double the quantities of all the ingredients except the cloves. It will keep for 2–3 weeks in a sealed jar in the refrigerator.

Veal Pot-au-Feu with Ginger

—

I have a weak spot for this wonderfully aromatic pot-au-feu. It's simpler, lighter, and quicker to make than the classic beef version and the broth is especially delectable, with or without the noodles. More than ever, the flavor will be dependent on the quality of your ingredients, so use the freshest and best you can get. You can prepare and cook the meat the night before and then finish cooking the dish the next day, straining the broth and adding the vegetables when you are ready to serve. Most importantly, don't be tempted to light scented candles for your pot-au-feu dinner party—instead let the aroma from the pot fill your home, and drift out of your front door to welcome your guests as they arrive.

Veal Pot-au-Feu with Ginger

Times

Active: 30 minutes
Cooking: about 2 hours

Serves 12
—

Ingredients

- 3 whole veal shanks
- 2 onions
- 4 cloves
- 2½ oz. (70 g) fresh ginger
- 4 lemongrass stalks (optional)
- 3 garlic cloves, unpeeled
- 2 tbsp mixed peppercorns
- 8½ cups (2 liters) My Chicken Broth (see recipe p. 118) (or 4 chicken bouillon cubes dissolved in 8½ cups/2 liters water)
- 12 sweet, crisp carrots
- 6 parsnips
- 12 leeks, white parts only
- 4 fennel bulbs
- Salt and freshly ground pepper

To serve
- 1 large tbsp per person of vermicelli noodles, cooked according to the package instructions (optional)
- Mustard, assorted pickles such as cornichons and baby onions, baby pattypan squash, and baby beets

Place the veal shanks side by side in 1 large or 2 medium Dutch ovens. Peel the onions and stud each with two cloves, peel and thinly slice the ginger, and quarter the lemongrass stalks (if using). Add the onions, garlic, ginger, peppercorns, and lemongrass to the pot(s), season with salt, and add enough chicken broth to just cover the veal shanks. Bring to a boil, cover, reduce the heat to very low, and cook for 1½ hours, or until the meat is fall-off-the-bones tender. Cook for an additional 15–20 minutes, if necessary.

Meanwhile, prepare the vegetables. Peel the carrots and parsnips. Remove the tough outer leaves from the leeks, wash them, and cut all three vegetables into 2-in. (5-cm) pieces, or leave them whole. Remove the tough outer leaves from the fennel and cut the bulbs into quarters.

Lift the meat out of the pot with a skimmer and transfer it to a large sauté pan. Add 3 ladlefuls of broth and strain the remaining broth through a fine-mesh sieve into a large saucepan—the broth should be perfectly clear. Discard the lemongrass and ginger. Add the carrots and parsnips to the broth and bring to a boil. Reduce to a simmer, cover, and cook for 10 minutes, then add the leeks and fennel. Cook for an additional 10 minutes, or until the vegetables are al dente. Using a skimmer, lift the vegetables out of the broth and place around the veal in the sauté pan, if the pan is large enough. If not, place the vegetables in a microwave-safe dish and reheat in the microwave with a ladleful of broth just before serving.

Taste the fragrant, clear broth and add more salt or pepper as necessary. If there is not enough to serve twelve people (about 24 ladlefuls), add more chicken broth or water. Serve the broth as a starter, with or without noodles.

For the second course, gently reheat the veal shanks and vegetables. Transfer the veal shanks, either whole or with the meat in large pieces (it should easily break apart with a spoon), to a large serving dish. Arrange the vegetables around the meat, or serve them separately. Accompany with mustard and assorted pickles in small dishes, as sides for guests to help themselves.

Duck Rillettes

No foods are taboo in this book, so I'm leaving it up to you to choose the recipes that suit you best. These rillettes, in the true French tradition, are neither too fatty, nor too dry, but moist, foolproof, and they keep well. If stored in an airtight terrine or mason jar on the upper shelf in the fridge, they'll last for two to three weeks—if you have any left over that is. As always, the flavor depends on the quality of the duck, so get yours from a trusted source. Spread thickly on toasted country bread, these rillettes are perfect for a light—or more substantial—snack, whether you're on your own or feeding a crowd.

Times

Active: 15 minutes
Cooking: 3–3½ hours

Serves about 20
—

Ingredients

- 1 whole duckling (about 4½ lb./2 kg), gutted
- 1 lb. (500 g) pork shoulder, cut into 6 large pieces
- 6 large shallots
- 2 bay leaves
- 2 thyme sprigs
- 3 cups (750 ml) water
- Salt and freshly ground pepper

To serve
- Cornichons
- Pickled pearl onions
- Country bread, plain or toasted
- A green salad

Preheat the oven to 300°F (150°C/Gas mark 2).

Rinse the duck and pork under cold water and place in a large Dutch oven (preferably cast iron). Peel and thinly slice the shallots. Add the shallots, bay leaves, and thyme to the pot and season with salt and pepper. Pour in the water and bring to a boil. Cover, transfer to the oven, and cook for 2 hours, turning the duck over halfway through the cooking time. After 2 hours, the duck legs should pull away easily, the meat should fall off the bones, and the pork will be very tender. If not, turn the duck over again, add a little more water, if necessary, and return to the oven for an additional 30 minutes.

Remove the pot from the oven. Carefully lift out the duck onto a cutting board (leaving the pork and shallots in the pot) and discard the bay leaves and thyme sprigs. When the duck is cool enough to handle, remove the skin and bones with your fingers, and discard.

Return the duck meat to the pot containing the very tender pork and the shallots, which will have melted into the reduced, but essential, cooking juices.

Stir with a wooden spatula to finely shred the meat. Set over low heat, cover, and cook for 1 hour, stirring occasionally. By now, the pan juices should be concentrated. If not, remove the lid and increase the heat to speed up the evaporation.

It's ready! All that remains is to transfer the rillettes to a terrine and serve either hot—my favorite—or leave until cold and then chill. Accompany with cornichons, pickled onions, country bread, and a green salad. Ah, *la vie est belle!*

Fruity Chicken Curry

When I'm short on ideas, this deliciously easy curry always comes to mind and ends up winning the day. The bright sunny color of the sauce and sweet-and-sour flavors will make it one of your go-to dishes, too. It's perfect for winter or summer, and Indian cuisine, unlike Japanese, is popular with all ages, both young and old. Another plus is that you can make it a day ahead, as it will taste even better the following day—if you can wait that long.

Times

Active: 30 minutes
Marinating: 30 minutes
Cooking: 40–45 minutes

Serves 12

—

Ingredients

- 4 limes
- 2 lb. (1 kg) chicken breasts
- 1⅔ cups (400 g) whole milk yogurt
- 2 Granny Smith apples
- 2 medium onions
- 1 green banana
- 1 mango
- 1 bunch cilantro
- 2 tbsp peanut oil
- 3 tbsp Madras curry powder
- 1 tsp ground ginger
- Salt and freshly ground pepper

To serve
- Standing Rice (see recipe p. 138)

Wash and dry the limes, grate the zest of one, and juice all four. Thinly slice the chicken breasts.

Place the zest and juice in a large bowl, add the chicken and yogurt, and stir to combine. Let marinate for 30 minutes in the refrigerator.

Peel and chop the apples and onions. Peel the banana and mango and cut into small dice or thin slices. Wash and dry the cilantro and finely chop the leaves, setting some aside for garnish.

Heat the oil in a large nonstick sauté pan (or two smaller pans) over high heat. Add the onions, curry powder, ginger, and fruit and cook for 5 minutes, stirring constantly. Lower the heat to medium, cover the pan(s), and let stew for 30 minutes, stirring occasionally. Add the chicken with its marinade, the cilantro, and season with salt and pepper. Stir constantly with two spatulas for 5–7 minutes or until the chicken is cooked. The curry is now ready to serve, but it can be cooled and then refrigerated until the following day, so the flavors develop even more. Reheat without boiling, just before serving, adding salt, pepper, and more lime juice as needed.

Garnish with the reserved chopped cilantro and accompany with Standing Rice, allowing about 2 oz. (60 g) per person. Serve, and be prepared for a happy table.

Notes

For a vegetarian dish, you can replace the chicken with vegetables of your choice.

Chicken Fricassee with Garlic and Vinegar

This richly flavored version of a great French classic was inspired by the late chef Joël Robuchon. It's perfect for sharing, whatever the time of year, and whether you're cooking for four or for ten. Like many of my favorite dishes for entertaining, it can be prepared a day ahead, right up to the final step.

Times

Make a day ahead
Active: 30 minutes
Cooking: 1 hour 10 minutes

Serves 12
—

Ingredients

- 4 tomatoes (about 1¼ lb./600 g)
- 4–5 sweet, crisp carrots, depending on size
- 3 tbsp (1¾ oz./50 g) butter
- 4 tbsp sunflower oil
- 2 chickens, preferably organic, weighing at least 3½ lb. (1.5 kg) each, jointed into 8 pieces (see Notes)
- 20 garlic cloves, unpeeled
- Scant 3 cups (700 ml) aged red wine vinegar
- 2 tbsp tomato paste
- 1 bouquet garni (4 bay leaves, 3 thyme sprigs, and 6 flat-leaf parsley sprigs, tied together with kitchen twine)
- ½ cup (125 ml) heavy cream
- 2 tbsp hot Dijon mustard
- 2 tbsp Cognac or Armagnac (optional)
- Salt and freshly ground pepper

To serve
- Fresh tarragon
- Tagliatelle or pasta shells tossed with butter

Peel and halve the tomatoes and remove the seeds. Peel the carrots and cut them into ½-in. (1-cm) rounds.

Place the butter and oil in a cast-iron Dutch oven, large enough to take all the chicken joints, and set over low heat. When the butter has melted, increase the heat to high, add the chicken pieces, and brown on all sides (about 5 minutes in total).

Add the carrots, garlic cloves, and vinegar and bring to a boil. Let boil for 5 minutes to allow some of the vinegar to evaporate. Partially cover the pot, lower to a simmer, and continue to reduce for 10 minutes. Add the tomatoes, tomato paste, and bouquet garni, and season with salt and pepper. Stir, cover, and cook over low heat for 45 minutes, or until the chicken is fall-off-the-bones tender. Remove the bouquet garni. You can make the fricassee up to this point a day ahead. Cool and refrigerate until ready to reheat and serve.

In a bowl, combine the heavy cream, mustard, and Cognac or Armagnac (if using). Season with salt and pepper, pour over the chicken in the pot, and let boil for 2 minutes. Serve immediately garnished with fresh tarragon and accompanied by buttered pasta. Mouthwateringly good!

Notes

Although good organic chicken makes this fricassee special, if you want something more unusual, use duck instead. If you do choose duck, count on serving eight rather than twelve people. Since duck is slightly fattier than chicken, after browning the meat for a good 5 minutes in the first step, drain the excess fat from the pan and discard it. Otherwise, proceed as indicated.

Braised Chicken with Saffron and Fennel

Since I was a child, I've loved eating crisp, raw fennel.
In this dish, the fennel is cooked but still retains its freshness
and infuses the chicken with its mild anise flavor. The
barberries, widely used in Persian cuisine, add a subtle tang
that is similar to sumac. I must thank Yotam Ottolenghi for
introducing me, not to this Moroccan dish with spices I'm
familiar with, but to these tiny, deep red berries that contrast
with the sweetness of the fennel. It's my favorite kind of dish:
generous but unfussy, and even better the next day. It might be
even tastier made with lamb or veal—something I'll have to try
soon. You and your loved ones will be transported to Isfahan—
with zero carbon footprint.

Times

Active: 30 minutes
Cooking: 1 ½–2 hours

Serves 12
—

Ingredients

- 4 large onions
- 4 tbsp extra-virgin olive oil
- 2 large chickens, preferably organic, weighing at least 3½ lb. (1.5 kg) each, jointed into 8 pieces
- 2 pinches saffron threads (too little is better than too much, as you can always add more later)
- 2 tbsp ground cumin
- 1 tsp ground cinnamon
- Juice of 2 oranges
- Juice of 2 lemons
- 3½ oz. (100 g) barberries
- 6 fennel bulbs
- 4 tbsp clear honey
- Fleur de sel and freshly ground pepper

To serve (optional)
- Persian Basmati Rice (see recipe p. 136)

Preheat the oven to 300°F (150°C/Gas mark 2). Peel and roughly chop the onions.

Place a pan of water in the base of the oven to create steam. As the chicken isn't submerged in liquid in the pot, steam from the water will help keep it flavorful and moist.

Heat the olive oil in a large Dutch oven over medium heat. Add the onions and sauté for 5 minutes, stirring constantly, until golden. Add the chicken pieces and let brown for several minutes, stirring nonstop with two spatulas. Reduce the heat to low.

Meanwhile, bring a small saucepan of water to a boil. Crush the saffron threads against the sides of a small bowl with the back of a spoon to make a powder (don't worry if a few threads remain). Pour 3 tablespoons boiling water over this precious spice to release its flavor, and then add the saffron and liquid to the chicken and onions. Fill the bowl that contained the saffron with more boiling water, stir to incorporate any remaining threads, and pour into the Dutch oven. Stir in the cumin, cinnamon, orange juice, and lemon juice, and season with fleur de sel and pepper. Bring to a boil, stir, cover, and transfer to the oven. After 1 hour, remove the pot and check the liquid level. If only a little liquid remains, add a small glassful of water.

If you want to serve the dish the next day, let it cool at this point and refrigerate overnight.

Rinse the barberries under hot water. Remove the stalks and outer leaves of the fennel and cut each bulb in half lengthwise. Add the barberries, fennel, and honey to the pot. Return to the oven for an additional 30 minutes.

Serve hot with Persian Basmati Rice, if desired. *Bon voyage!*

Cod Blanquette

If you are a gourmet who is pressed for time and an inept cook, this recipe is for you. If you are an experienced cook and a gourmet, have fun tonight making this dish for friends! If you don't have any cod or similar white fish, you can still make the sauce, as it's marvelous served over all sorts of things, such as lentils, basmati rice, quinoa, or tagliatelle. If you prefer a romantic dinner for two, divide everything by four, apart from the candles on the table as they will cast a flattering light.

Times

Active: 30 minutes
Cooking: 12–15 minutes

Serves 10
—

Ingredients

- 2 bunches sorrel (if not in season, use more spinach)
- 14 oz. (400 g) chopped frozen spinach, thawed (or 2 lb./1 kg fresh spinach)
- 2 bunches flat-leaf parsley
- 2 bunches chervil
- ½ bunch chives
- 4 tarragon sprigs (see Notes)
- 4 basil sprigs (see Notes)
- 2 tbsp butter
- 4 tbsp extra-virgin olive oil
- 2½ cups (600 ml) low-fat evaporated milk
- 1 tsp ground turmeric or curry powder (whichever you prefer)
- 1¼ lb. (600 g) short-grain rice (preferably from the Camargue), black rice, or tagliatelle
- 3½ lb. (1.5 kg) cod fillet, cut into 10 pieces (or another white fish of your choice)
- Juice of 3 lemons
- Salt and freshly ground pepper

Wash the sorrel and fresh spinach (if using), remove the leaves from the tough stems, and slice thinly. If you are using frozen spinach, you've gained 15 minutes. Wash and dry the herbs and roughly chop the leaves, reserving a few chervil leaves for garnish.

Heat the butter and oil in two sauté pans or a large Dutch oven over medium heat. Add the sorrel and spinach and cook for about 5 minutes, tossing constantly with two spatulas, until wilted.

Season with salt, add the evaporated milk, turmeric or curry powder, and herbs, and cook, uncovered, for 5 minutes. Season generously with pepper. You can make the sauce up to this point a day ahead, refrigerating it once it has cooled, but wait until serving before adding the fish.

When ready to serve, cook the rice or pasta according to the package instructions. Bring the sauce to a simmer and add the fish. Reduce the heat to low, cover, and cook for 2 minutes, or until the fish is opaque and the flesh flakes easily. Gently stir in the lemon juice.

Garnish with the reserved chervil and serve with the rice or pasta to soak up the wonderful sauce.

Notes

The tarragon and basil can be replaced with other herbs of your choice, such as cilantro or dill.

Monkfish Carina

This Italian recipe is one of my favorites. It's as quick to make whether you're cooking for four or for ten, and is full of flavor, is pretty to look at (the meaning of "carina" in Italian), and is always a hit. Monkfish is ideal because even after the backbone has been removed, its firm flesh holds its shape when cut into thin slices. I'll share a little secret with you: if you ask your fishmonger nicely, he'll prepare the fish for you in minutes. Otherwise, with the help of a good knife, it's easy to do.

Times
Active: 30 minutes
Cooking: 15 minutes

Serves 10
—

Ingredients
- 2½ lb. (1.2 kg) monkfish fillet
- All-purpose flour, for dredging
- 10 cherry tomatoes
- 4 tbsp extra-virgin olive oil, divided
- 1 stick (4 oz./120 g) butter, diced
- ½ cup (1 oz./25 g) chopped fresh parsley
- 1 cup (250 ml) strained tomatoes (passata)
- 4 tbsp finely chopped cornichons
- 3 tbsp drained capers (optional)
- A few drops Worcestershire sauce
- Juice of 2 lemons
- Salt and freshly ground pepper

Preheat the oven to 350°F (180°C/Gas mark 4).

Rinse the monkfish, remove any skin, dry on paper towels, and cut into ten slices. Place the flour in a shallow dish and coat the fish with it, shaking off any excess. Wash and roughly chop the cherry tomatoes.

In a large nonstick skillet, heat 2 tablespoons of the olive oil over high heat. Add the monkfish slices in a single layer (you may need to do this in batches) and cook for 2 minutes on each side until golden. As they turn golden, remove the fish slices with a skimmer and transfer to a plate.

Pour the oil out of the skillet and wipe it clean. Return it to high heat, add the butter, the remaining olive oil, cherry tomatoes, and parsley, reserving a little of the parsley for garnish. Cook for 30 seconds, stir in the strained tomatoes, cornichons, capers (if using), Worcestershire sauce, and lemon juice. Season with salt and pepper, bring to a simmer, add the monkfish, and heat through.

Scatter over the reserved parsley and serve at once.

So delicious, so *carina!*

Patricia's Crème Caramel

For me, crème caramel is the ultimate comfort food. It's like a cozy blanket and is perfect for all occasions, no matter who is gathered around the table. My friend Patricia's crème caramel is always flawless—including the unmolding—but it's hard to resist a second helping. If you're serving more than eight, it's best to make two rather than double the quantities of ingredients.

Times
Active: 25 minutes
Cooking: 40 minutes

Serves 8
—

Ingredients

For the caramel
- 3 tbsp water
- 1¼ cups (9 oz./250 g) sugar

For the custard
- 4 cups (1 liter) whole milk
- 1 Madagascan or Tahitian vanilla bean (or ½ tsp ground vanilla bean)
- 6 eggs
- ¼ cup (1¾ oz./50 g) superfine sugar

Preheat the oven to 350°F (180°C/Gas mark 4).

Prepare the caramel by putting the water and sugar in a saucepan set over high heat. Swirl the pan occasionally until the sugar dissolves and then boil until the syrup turns a deep amber color. Pour immediately into a 9-in. (23-cm) porcelain soufflé dish and tilt the dish to coat the bottom and sides. Immediately put the saucepan to soak in hot water—this will make it easier to clean.

To prepare the custard, pour the milk into a saucepan. Split the vanilla bean lengthwise and scrape the seeds into the milk, adding the bean as well, or add the vanilla powder (if using). Bring to a boil, remove from the heat, cover, and let infuse for several minutes before removing the bean.

Whisk the eggs in a mixing bowl. Slowly pour in the hot milk, stirring slowly but continuously with the whisk to avoid creating froth. If there is any, remove it with a skimmer.

Pour the custard into the dish over the caramel and carefully lift it into a roasting pan. Pour in enough water to come halfway up the sides of the dish. Bake for 30 minutes, watching closely as the water should reach a gentle simmer without either the custard or the water coming to a boil. If this happens, lower the oven temperature to 325°F (170°C/Gas mark 3).

Carefully remove the roasting pan from the oven and lift the soufflé dish out of the pan. Let the crème caramel cool to room temperature, and then either turn it out into a serving dish or serve it directly from the soufflé dish. Dust with superfine sugar.

Arthur's Chocolate Gâteau

I've dedicated a cake (their favorite) to each of my grandchildren. Arthur is my oldest grandchild and he chose my chocolate gâteau to be named after him.

Times

Active: 25 minutes
Cooking: 22–25 minutes

Serves 8
—

Ingredients

- 10½ oz. (300 g) dark chocolate, 70% cacao
- 3 tbsp black coffee (or 1 tsp instant coffee dissolved in 3 tbsp boiling water)
- 1¾ sticks (7 oz./200 g) salted butter, thinly sliced and softened
- 5 eggs
- 1⅓ cups (6 oz./180 g) confectioners' sugar, divided, plus extra for dredging

To serve
- Crème Anglaise (see recipe p. 193)

Remove a rack from the oven and preheat the oven to 300°F (150°C/Gas mark 2). Stand a 9½-in. (24-cm) nonstick shallow cake pan (preferably silicone) on the rack to make it easier to transfer to the oven when filled with cake batter.

Chop the chocolate into small pieces and place in a microwave-safe bowl with the coffee and butter. Microwave on full power for 1 minute to melt the butter and partially melt the chocolate, making sure the mixture doesn't boil. There will still be some half-melted pieces of chocolate, so work it with a spatula until they melt and the chocolate is perfectly smooth. Alternatively, you can melt the chocolate, coffee, and butter together in a saucepan over low heat, stirring constantly with a spatula until smooth.

Separate the eggs, placing the yolks in one large bowl and the whites in another. Add ¾ cup (3½ oz./100 g) of the confectioners' sugar to the egg yolks and whisk with an electric beater until pale and foamy. Wash and dry the beaters, and then whip the whites with the remaining confectioners' sugar until firm peaks form. Whisk the melted chocolate mixture into the egg yolks until smooth. Using a spatula, gradually fold in the whites until no streaks remain, taking care not to deflate them.

Pour the batter into the pan, slide the rack back into the oven, and bake for 22–25 minutes until the cake is set but still soft in the center.

If you have used a nonstick rather than a silicone pan, let the cake cool for 20 minutes before turning it out onto a serving plate. Let cool to room temperature. If you have used silicone, let the cake cool in the pan, and turn it out when ready to serve. The cake can be left at room temperature for several hours but do not refrigerate it. At the last minute, dust the cake with confectioners' sugar and serve with Crème Anglaise.

Ginger, Lime, and Honey Mangoes

The most difficult part of this otherwise simple dish is finding the perfect mangoes, which should feel heavy and be fully ripe. When mangoes are at their best, you can't go wrong with this lovely dessert, as it is refreshing and fragrant. Don't be tempted to make it too often, though, as you may tire of it, and that would be a pity!

Times

Active: 25 minutes
Cooking: 2 minutes
Chilling: at least 2 hours

Serves 12
—

Ingredients

- 4 perfectly ripe mangoes (1¼ lb./600 g each)
- 4 limes
- 2½ oz. (70 g) fresh ginger
- 6 tbsp acacia honey

Peel the mangoes, cut the flesh away from the pit, and then cut lengthwise into ½-in. (1-cm) thick slices. Arrange attractively on a serving dish. Wash and dry the limes. Finely grate the zest of one lime and juice all four. Peel and finely grate the ginger.

In a small saucepan, combine the lime zest, lime juice, ginger, and honey, and bring to a boil. Boil for 2 minutes and then pour over the mango slices. Cool and chill for at least 2 hours to allow the flavors to develop. Remove from the refrigerator 1 hour before serving.

Chocolate Marquise

You will be impressed by the respectful silence that falls when your guests taste a slice of this chocolate heaven. My suggestion for the host or hostess is to have a second helping, even if it's just a sliver, as your guests, who may not have dared to ask, will then feel free to do the same. A drizzle of Crème Anglaise takes this marquise to another level.

Times
Make a day ahead
Active: 30 minutes
Chilling: overnight

Serves 10
—

Ingredients

- 2 oz. (60 g) Theo's Meringues (see recipe p. 238) (or store-bought)
- 15 speculaas or petit-beurre cookies
- 9 oz. (250 g) dark chocolate, maximum 60% cacao
- 1 stick plus 1 tbsp (4½ oz./130 g) best-quality lightly salted butter
- 3 eggs
- ½ cup (125 ml) cold black coffee
- Scant ½ cup (2 oz./60 g) unsweetened cocoa powder

CRÈME ANGLAISE

Times
Active: 25 minutes
Cooking: 20 minutes
Infusing: 15 minutes
Chilling: at least 2 hours

Serves 10
—

Ingredients

- 4 cups (1 liter) whole milk
- 2 Madagascan or Tahitian vanilla beans (or a few coffee beans, for coffee crème anglaise)
- 14 egg yolks
- 1¼ cups (9 oz./250 g) sugar

Line a 10 × 4-in. (26 × 10-cm) silicone loaf pan (or metal pan or disposable aluminum pan) with plastic wrap, leaving enough overhanging to cover the marquise after filling the pan. Roughly crush the meringues between your fingers, chop the cookies into ½-in. (1-cm) pieces, and place both in a bowl. Chop the dark chocolate, dice the butter, and lightly beat the eggs.

Place the coffee, chocolate, and butter in a large saucepan. Stir constantly over low heat with a wooden spatula until the butter has melted and the chocolate has nearly melted, without letting the mixture boil. Remove from the heat and stir in the cocoa powder until smooth. Let cool for 10 minutes. Using a spatula, beat the eggs into the chocolate mixture until well combined. Lightly fold in the crushed meringues and cookie pieces.

Pour into the prepared pan, spread the top level, and fold the overhanging plastic wrap over the top. Chill the marquise overnight in the refrigerator.

Turn out the marquise onto a serving plate 15 minutes before serving. Slice and serve with a drizzle of Crème Anglaise.

Crème anglaise

Put the milk in a large saucepan, slit the vanilla beans lengthwise and scrape the seeds into the milk, adding the beans as well (or add the coffee beans, if using). Bring to a boil, remove from the heat, and cover. Let infuse for 15 minutes (15–30 minutes for the coffee beans) and then remove the beans.

Chill a large metal spoon in the refrigerator to test the custard. In a large bowl, whisk the egg yolks and sugar together until pale and thick. Slowly drizzle in the infused milk, whisking constantly. Pour it back into the saucepan and stir constantly with a wooden spatula (making figure of eight movements is less tedious), over low heat for 15–20 minutes, until the custard thickens and coats the spatula. It is important not to let the custard boil or the egg yolks will scramble. Remove it from the heat and stir for a few more minutes. Dip the chilled spoon into the custard to coat the back of it, draw a line down the center with your fingertip, and if the line holds, the custard is ready. If not, cook for a few more minutes and test again but do this frequently as an undercooked custard will be too runny and an overcooked one will curdle.

Pour into an attractive serving bowl or jug and press plastic wrap over the surface to prevent a skin forming. Let cool and chill for at least 2 hours.

Little Coffee Custards

*If, like me, you're a coffee fan, you'll love these little custards,
which make the perfect finale after a main course
of Veal Pot-au-Feu with Ginger (see recipe p. 173)
or Nine Vegetable Shortcut Couscous (see recipe p. 128).
If you eat one custard, you'll feel satisfied and light.
Beyond that, I couldn't possibly say.*

Times

Active: 20 minutes
Cooking: 40–45 minutes

Makes 12 × 5-oz. (150-ml) porcelain custard cups
—

Ingredients

- 3⅓ cups (800 ml) whole milk
- ¾ cup (200 ml) heavy cream
- 4 tbsp instant decaf coffee granules
- 10 egg yolks
- 1 cup (7 oz./200 g) sugar

Heat the milk and cream in a saucepan over low heat and stir in the instant coffee until dissolved. Remove from the heat and let cool slightly.

Preheat the oven to 350°F (180°C/Gas mark 4). Line the base of a baking dish large enough to hold the twelve custard cups with aluminum foil.

In a mixing bowl (preferably with a spout), whisk the egg yolks and sugar together until pale and thick. Gradually pour in the coffee-infused milk and cream, stirring gently with the whisk to avoid creating froth.

Place the empty custard cups in the prepared baking dish and pour enough hot water into the dish to reach halfway up the sides of the cups.

Slowly fill the custard cups to within ½ in. (1 cm) of the tops, trying not to create air bubbles as you do so. If there are any bubbles, burst them with the tip of a knife or remove them with a teaspoon, so the custards will be smooth and shiny on top when cooked. If you leave them, little craters will form on the surface, which isn't very appetizing.

Cover the custard cups with a sheet of aluminum foil and cook for 40–45 minutes, checking occasionally to make sure the custards are not boiling. You'll know they are ready when they are set but still have a slight wobble.

Remove the baking dish from the oven and, taking care not to burn yourself, lift out the custard cups, and let cool to room temperature. Once the custards are no longer warm, you can chill them in the refrigerator.

Serve chilled or at room temperature.

Rice Pudding

There's no better pick-me-up than a sweet, comforting rice pudding. I tried many recipes before fine-tuning this one and I'm delighted to be able to share it with you. You can proceed with confidence, keeping in mind that the quality of your ingredients does at least half the work. Using short-grain rice (but not risotto rice) is the key to a creamy result and the best—in my opinion—comes from Italy or the Camargue in southern France. As for the best vanilla, it comes from Madagascar or Tahiti. Not very locavore, I know, unless you can grow the seeds on your balcony!

Times

Make a day ahead, if possible
Active: 45 minutes
Cooking: 30 minutes
Chilling: 3–4 hours (or overnight)

Serves 10
—

Ingredients

- 3 quarts (3 liters) water
- 2½ cups (1 lb./500 g) short-grain rice (also known as round-grain or pudding rice)
- 10 cups (2.5 liters) whole milk
- 1 pinch salt
- 2 Madagascan or Tahitian vanilla beans
- 8 egg yolks (see Notes)
- 1¼ cups (8½ oz./240 g) sugar
- 7 tbsp (3½ oz./100 g) salted butter

Bring the water to a boil in a large pot. Add the rice, return to a boil, and cook for 4 minutes. Drain and set aside. In the same pot, heat the milk with a pinch of salt over low heat. Split the vanilla beans lengthwise and scrape the seeds into the milk, adding the beans as well. When the milk begins to simmer, add the rice, and cook over low heat for 20–25 minutes, stirring toward the end to prevent any grains sticking to the bottom of the pot. The rice must be tender but the grains still separate. Remove from the heat and carefully lift out the vanilla beans.

Whisk the egg yolks and sugar together with an electric beater until pale and foamy. Switch to a wooden spatula and stir the mixture into the rice. Dice the butter and stir in until well blended.

Divide the rice pudding between two deep 8-in. (20-cm) soufflé dishes and press plastic wrap over the surface to prevent a skin forming. Refrigerate for at least 3–4 hours or preferably overnight, as the pudding will be even more delicious the following day. I take mine out of the refrigerator about 1 hour before serving to ensure we enjoy it at its best.

Notes

Unlike yolks, egg whites freeze well. Store unused egg whites in an airtight container and defrost when needed, to make Theo's Meringues (see recipe p. 238) for your next party, for instance.

Tarte Tatin

—

This tart is special. However, it was the result of a careless mistake by the Tatin sisters, who ran a small traditional French hotel in the village of Lamotte-Beuvron in the late nineteenth century. The tart immortalized them and has gifted us a marvelous dessert, which, although not the lightest, is certainly the most delicious. As the story goes, one of the sisters was making her customary apple tart but forgot the crust. As the apples baked in the pan, a caramelized aroma drifted through the kitchen and, realizing her mistake, she covered the apples with the forgotten dough, and returned the pan to the oven. The scent that escaped as the tart was turned out offered a hint of the treat to come: tender, caramelized apples and a crisp, golden crust. The legend—and recipe—was born.

Tarte Tatin

Times
Active: 40 minutes
Cooking: 1 hour

Serves 8 (make 2 tarts if you have more guests)

—

Ingredients

**For the pastry crust
(all the ingredients must be at room temperature)**
- 1½ cups (6¼ oz./180 g) all-purpose flour
- 6 tbsp (3 oz./90 g) salted butter, diced
- 1 tbsp superfine sugar
- 3 tbsp water

For the filling
- 1 lemon
- 3½ lb. (1.5 kg) slightly tart apples, such as King of the Pippins or Granny Smith
- 7 tbsp (3½ oz./100 g) salted butter, diced
- ⅔ cup (4½ oz./125 g) sugar
- Scant 2 tsp vanilla sugar
- ½ tsp ground cinnamon

To decorate
- Toasted sesame seeds

To prepare the pastry crust, fit a stand mixer with the dough hook or make the pastry by hand. Quickly combine all of the ingredients into a rough dough with small lumps of butter remaining to ensure the crust remains flaky when baked. Shape into a disk, cover with plastic wrap, and chill in the refrigerator. **Preheat the oven** to 400°F (210°C/Gas mark 6).

To prepare the filling, wash and dry the lemon, finely grate the zest, and squeeze the juice. Set aside. Peel the apples and cut them in half from top to bottom, removing the cores and seeds.

Place the butter and sugar in the base of a 9-in. (22-cm) burner-safe round cake pan (not loose-based) or oven-safe skillet, 2–2½ in. (5–6 cm) deep. Set over high heat. When the sugar melts and the mixture turns golden, wear oven mitts to lift the pan off the heat and carefully tilt it from side to side to coat the base with caramel. Arrange the apples tightly together over the caramel, cut sides up, and sprinkle with the vanilla sugar, cinnamon, lemon juice, and zest.

Bake the apples for 20–30 minutes until they are tender and caramelized. Remove the pan from the oven and let cool slightly, leaving the oven switched on.

Remove the dough from the refrigerator and roll it to a thickness of ¼ in. (5 mm). Lift the dough over the apples, tucking the edges down inside the pan, as if you were tucking in a bedsheet.

Bake for 25–30 minutes, until the pastry is crisp and golden. Let cool in the pan for 10 minutes, run a spatula around the edges between the pastry and the tin, and turn the tart out onto a serving plate. If you are serving it right away, lift off the pan, sprinkle with toasted sesame seeds, and take it to the table. Otherwise, leave the pan on top of the tart until just before serving to prevent the apples from slipping off the sides.

The tart can be served hot or warm, but never cold.

Tiramisu

Until recently, I refused to try tiramisu under the pretext that it was made with mascarpone and I'm not a cheese eater. But with age, the mind mellows, and one day I found myself lifting a spoonful of tiramisu to my lips, only to discover the pure delight without the faintest cheese flavor. Since that first taste, I've made tiramisu many times and I eat it to my heart's content. There's no turning back now! In my opinion, it is the best Italian dessert there is, as long as you use a top-quality mascarpone. Make your tiramisu a day ahead for even better results.

Times

Make a day ahead
Active: 25 minutes
Cooking: 10 minutes
Resting: 4 hours–overnight

Serves 10
—

Ingredients

For the cookie base
- 3 tbsp (1¾ oz./50 g) salted butter, plus extra for greasing
- 7 oz. (200 g) speculaas or petit-beurre cookies
- 1 tbsp sugar

For the mascarpone cream
- 3 eggs
- Scant ½ cup (3 oz./80 g) sugar
- Generous 1 cup (9 oz./250 g) mascarpone
- Scant ½ cup (3½ oz./100 g) crème fraîche (or heavy cream)
- 2 pinches Madagascan or Tahitian ground vanilla bean

To assemble
- 1 cup (250 ml) cold strong black coffee (or 1 generous tbsp instant decaf coffee dissolved in 1 cup/250 ml water)
- 3 tbsp amaretto liqueur (or rum)
- 30 ladyfingers
- 2 tbsp unsweetened cocoa powder
- 3½ oz. (100 g) dark chocolate, 70% cacao

To prepare the cookie base, preheat the oven to 300°F (150°C/Gas mark 2) and grease a large round or oval glass baking dish with butter. In the bowl of a food processor, pulse the 3 tablespoons butter, cookies, and sugar together until you obtain coarse crumbs that stick together. Transfer to the baking dish and press over the base in an even layer with the palm of your hand. Bake for 10 minutes and then let cool.

To prepare the mascarpone cream, separate the eggs, putting the yolks in one large bowl and the whites in another. Add the sugar, mascarpone, crème fraiche or heavy cream, and vanilla to the yolks and whisk until well combined.

Whisk the egg whites with an electric beater until firm peaks form. Gently fold the whites into the yolk mixture with a spatula.

Spread a thin layer of the mascarpone cream over the cookie base.

Combine the coffee and liqueur in a shallow bowl and quickly dip half the ladyfingers in the mixture one at a time, until they are soaked but not falling apart. Arrange the ladyfingers side by side over the mascarpone cream.

Spread half the remaining mascarpone cream over the ladyfingers and dust with half the cocoa powder. Cover with the remaining ladyfingers dipped into the coffee mixture as before, and top with the remaining mascarpone cream. Smooth over the cream with a spatula and dust with a final layer of cocoa powder.

Chill in the refrigerator for at least 4 hours or, better still, overnight.

Just before serving, use a vegetable peeler to shave off flakes of dark chocolate. Sprinkle these over the tiramisu in a final flourish worthy of the great *pâtissière* you are. Wow factor guaranteed!

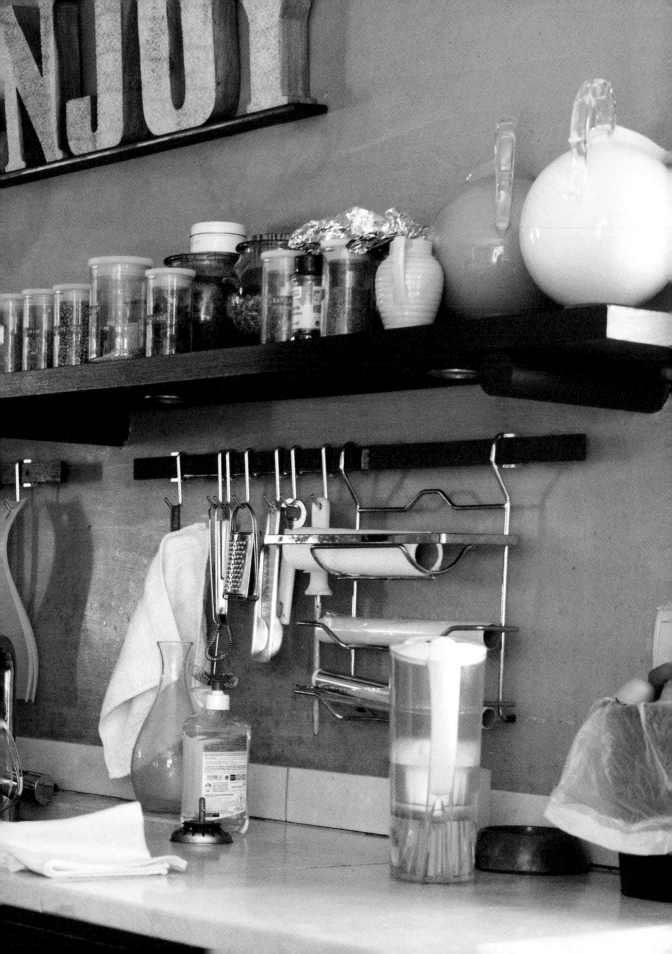

all year round

Cocktail Hour Refreshments

Bread

Teatime Treats

Black Meddoh

Élyane, a journalist friend of mine and a raw food expert, gave me this recipe and I haven't changed it a bit. It has since become a favorite accompaniment to aperitifs and, in Provence, has even ousted tapenade from its throne. As I write this, I realize that I never think to make my Black Meddoh during the winter in Paris—and what a mistake! This is soon to be remedied, though, much to the delight of my Parisian friends. When you serve Black Meddoh, turn it into a guessing game as, at my house, no one has been able to determine the exact mix of ingredients that goes into this irresistible appetizer.

Times

Active: 15 minutes
Soaking: 10–15 minutes

Serves 12
—

Ingredients

- 60 pitted black Greek olives
- 8 sweet, plump, pitted medjool dates
- 8 sundried tomatoes
- 2 pink garlic cloves
- 3 tbsp extra-virgin olive oil
- *Piment d'Espelette* (to taste)

To garnish
- Toasted sesame seeds

To serve
- Grissini, Spiced Flatbread (see recipe p. 216–17), or another favorite bread

Soak the olives and dates in hot water for 10–15 minutes. Drain and roughly chop with the sundried tomatoes. Peel the garlic cloves and remove the germs.

Place all the ingredients in the bowl of a food processor and pulse into a coarse puree.

Divide the black meddoh between two serving bowls and refrigerate. Let it come to room temperature before serving, so the flavors are bolder and even harder to guess.

Serve sprinkled with toasted sesame seeds and accompany with grissini, Spiced Flatbread, or another favorite bread.

Notes

If you want to have a small supply of black meddoh on hand, double the quantities of ingredients and store in the refrigerator in an airtight container, where it will keep for several months.

Ginger-Lemongrass Infusion

You can serve this invigorating drink hot in winter or well chilled in summer. As everyone loves it, you'll end up making 3 quarts (3 liters) at a time, like me, so you always have some in the refrigerator. Is it necessary to remind ourselves of all the health benefits that ginger provides? Antibacterial, antiviral, energy-giving, digestion-aiding, and aphrodisiac, to name but a few. If you drink this first thing in the morning on an empty stomach, you'll maximize its effect but, no matter what time of day it is, I think you'll agree that this good-for-you drink is just plain good.

Times

Active: 20 minutes
Cooking: 1 hour
Chilling: 2 hours or longer

Makes 3 quarts (3 liters)

—

Ingredients

- 3 quarts (3 liters) water
- 4 oz. (120 g) fresh ginger
- 2 lemongrass stalks
- 3 tbsp honey of your choice
- Juice of 4 limes

Bring the water to a boil in a large pot. Meanwhile, peel and cut or grate the ginger into thin slices and quarter the lemongrass stalks. Add the ginger and lemongrass to the pot, and reduce the heat to very low. Cover the pot to limit the amount of water that evaporates, which would make the drink unnecessarily spicy, and simmer very gently for 1 hour.

Strain through a fine sieve into another pot or a large bowl. Discard the lemongrass and ginger and stir in the honey until dissolved. Taste and add more honey, if you wish. Let cool, then stir in the lime juice. Taste and add more honey or lime juice as needed. Using a funnel, pour the drink into three 4-cup (1-liter) bottles and chill for at least 2 hours to allow the flavors to develop.

Za'atar Man'ouche (Lebanese Pizza)

What a discovery! I like nothing better than simple, authentic foods that are not only delicious but within the reach of all budgets. This rustic Lebanese flatbread is one and it was my Lebanese friend Djenane who took me to try it in Beirut. Seated in front of a little stall run by a man named Aj, I had my first revelatory bite. Aj arrives every morning at 4 a.m. to prepare his dough and he begins selling man'ouche at dawn; as the French are enjoying their croissants, Beirut's residents are biting into their man'ouches. Ever since, I've been making my own at home. As simple as it is fragrant, za'atar man'ouche is very popular served with an aperitif. I must try it for breakfast, too; made with herbs, sesame seeds, and olive oil, it couldn't be healthier. It fills the house with an irresistible aroma while it is baking and it never fails to please.

Times

Active: 10 minutes
Rising: 1 hour
Cooking: 15 minutes

Makes 12–15 portions

Ingredients

- Scant 2 cups (8 oz./230 g) all-purpose flour
- 1 tbsp instant yeast
- 1 tsp sugar
- Generous ¾ cup (200 ml) lukewarm water
- ½ tsp salt
- 2 tbsp extra-virgin olive oil, plus extra for greasing and drizzling
- 3 tbsp za'atar (or oregano)
- 2 tbsp sesame seeds
- 1 pinch Cayenne pepper (optional)
- Fleur de sel

In the bowl of a stand mixer fitted with the dough hook, mix together half the flour with the yeast, sugar, and water on high speed. Cover and let rise for 30 minutes at room temperature in a draft-free place (a turned-off oven is ideal).

Add the remaining flour, salt, and olive oil and knead until smooth. Lightly grease your hands with olive oil and use to press out the dough in an even layer over the base of an 8 × 12-in. (20 × 30-cm) shallow baking pan. Sprinkle over the za'atar, sesame seeds, fleur de sel, and Cayenne pepper (if using). Drizzle with olive oil.

Let rise again for 30 minutes at room temperature, away from any drafts.

Preheat the oven to 325°F (170°C/Gas mark 3) and bake for about 15 minutes until golden.

Cut into 2-in. (5-cm) squares in the pan and serve warm on paper napkins. Finger food doesn't get better than this!

Avocado Puree

Perfect for large gatherings, this avocado puree is not a chunky dip like guacamole, but rather a silky treat in its own right, to be eaten with a small spoon or scooped up with grissini while sipping an aperitif. It makes a lovely sauce for Kuku (Iranian Herb Fritters, see recipe p. 218) and I've also recently discovered that it is sublime with roasted or steamed fish, particularly if enhanced with fresh herbs and purslane when it is in season. Smooth, creamy, and a pretty pastel green, this is a feast for the eyes and the taste buds. It's healthy and children love it, too.

Times
Active: 15 minutes

Serves 12
—

Ingredients
- 4 or 5 large ripe avocados
- 2 tbsp capers (or 10 small cornichons in vinegar) (optional)
- Juice of 2 or 3 lemons, depending on their size
- 5 tbsp fruity olive oil
- 6 tbsp finely chopped fresh herbs of your choice, such as parsley, basil, cilantro, and tarragon
- Salt and freshly ground pepper

Halve, pit, peel, and dice the avocados. Place in a blender with the capers (if using), lemon juice, olive oil, and 5 tablespoons of the fresh herbs. Season with salt and pepper and puree until smooth. Taste and add more salt, pepper, or lemon juice, as needed. If using cornichons instead of capers, cut them into thin slices and mix into the puree with a fork.

Spoon the puree into a large bowl, sprinkle with the remaining herbs, and serve at room temperature to best appreciate the flavors.

Spiced Flatbread

This spiced flatbread is a revelation when served with Black Meddoh (see recipe p. 209) at cocktail hour, or as part of a meze spread for lunch or dinner. After one bite, you'll be hooked, as, not only is it wonderfully fragrant and seemingly very light, it is actually as rich as brioche or naan but much easier to make. So, dive in and you'll be rewarded. One summer's day, when I had almost twenty over for lunch, I served two of these flatbreads with eight meze (or various salads—you'll find the recipes for many in this book), followed by Strawberry, Ginger, and Honey Compote (see recipe p. 106) and coffee. I only serve cooked fruit for dessert, as it's easier to digest and more luxurious.

Times
Active: 15 minutes
Resting: 1¾ hours
Cooking: 25–30 minutes

Serves 12
—

Ingredients

- 1½ cups (5¼ oz./150 g) crème fraîche or heavy cream
- Juice of 1 lemon
- ⅔ cup (150 ml) cold water
- Scant ½ cup (100 ml) boiling water
- 1 tbsp fleur de sel
- 2 tbsp sugar
- 1 tbsp instant yeast (or ⅔ oz./20 g fresh yeast)
- 3¼ cups (14 oz./400 g) all-purpose flour
- 1¾ cups (7 oz./200 g) whole wheat flour
- 3 tbsp cumin seeds
- 1 tbsp ground coriander
- 1 pinch salt
- 1 pinch red pepper flakes (optional)
- About ¾ cup (200 ml) extra-virgin olive oil, for greasing and brushing
- 1 tbsp dried thyme
- 1 tsp nigella seeds
- 1 tbsp sesame seeds
- 1 tbsp sumac

Preheat the oven to 120°F (50°C/Gas at its lowest possible temperature). In the bowl of a stand mixer fitted with the dough hook, quickly combine the cream with 1 teaspoon of the lemon juice and the cold and boiling water. Incorporate the fleur de sel and sugar. If using instant yeast, stir it into the all-purpose flour; if using fresh yeast, rub it into the flour. Add it to the bowl with the whole wheat flour, cumin, coriander, and red pepper flakes (if using), and mix to make a dough.

Knead until the dough forms a ball. Cover the bowl with a thin dish towel, turn the oven off, and place the dough inside. Let rest for 15 minutes. Meanwhile, grease and line a rimmed baking sheet with parchment paper or brush it generously with some of the olive oil.

Transfer the dough to the baking sheet. Grease your hands with olive oil and press down on the dough with your fingers to stretch it into a rectangle measuring approximately 16 × 10 in. (40 × 25 cm).

With your fingertips poke dimples into the surface of the dough. Cover with plastic wrap and let rest for 1½ hours in a draft-free spot. Near the end of the rising time, preheat the oven to 400°F (210°C/Gas mark 6).

Remove the plastic wrap and brush the surface of the dough, including the dimples, generously with the remaining olive oil. Sprinkle with the fleur de sel, thyme, seeds, and sumac.

Bake for 25–30 minutes, until golden. Be patient—the wait is nearly over. Remove from the oven, let the flatbread cool on a cooling rack, and then dig in.

Notes
All the spices and seeds can be replaced with others, according to your personal preference or the contents of your store cupboard.

Kuku (Iranian Herb Fritters)

Marjane Satrapi, the talented French-Iranian graphic novelist and film director, is a fan of these herb fritters (called Kuku in Farsi), which she serves with a garlic-yogurt dipping sauce. But beware—you won't be able to stop eating them! If, like me, you serve them as an appetizer with aperitifs, be generous with the number you make, and make sure the lunch or dinner to follow is light.

Times

Active: 30 minutes
Cooking: 10 minutes

Serves 8
—

Ingredients

For the garlic-yogurt sauce (see Notes)
- 2 pink garlic cloves
  (or 3½ oz./100 g *mousir*, dried Persian shallots, soaked in cold water for 3–4 hours, then drained)
- 2 cups (1 lb./500 g) regular or Greek-style plain yogurt

For the herb fritters (see Notes)
- 1 bunch parsley
- 1 bunch cilantro
- 1 bunch dill
- 2 onions
- 6 eggs
- 1 tbsp all-purpose flour
- ½ cup (125 ml) peanut oil, divided

To prepare the garlic-yogurt sauce, peel the garlic cloves and remove the germs. Crush with a garlic press (or mince the *mousir*) and stir into the yogurt. Cover and refrigerate.

To prepare the herb fritters, wash, dry, and roughly chop the herbs. Peel and roughly chop the onions. Place the herbs and onions in the bowl of a food processor and pulse until finely chopped but not reduced to a paste.

Whisk the eggs in a large bowl and then whisk in the flour and 2 tablespoons of the oil. Stir in the onion-herb mixture.

Heat the remaining oil in a large skillet over medium-high heat and line a large plate with paper towel. Using a tablespoon, add mounds of batter to the hot oil and cook for 1 minute on each side, until lightly golden. Drain on the plate so the paper towel absorbs the excess oil.

Serve hot with the chilled garlic-yogurt sauce.

Notes

For a refreshing alternative to the garlic-flavored sauce, grate one-third of a cucumber and stir it into the yogurt in place of the garlic. Chill and serve as indicated.

You can add other favorite herbs to the fritter batter, if you wish.

"Naanizza"

—

This is the story of an unlikely alliance. My "Les Roulades" friends and I (we are four foodies) share a passion for pizza but, sadly, we're often disappointed and rarely excited by the ones we try. So, my friends issued me with a challenge: invent a pizza. I took up the challenge in my kitchen in Provence in the summer of 2018, where I combined two things I love: naan—the Indian flatbread traditionally made in a tandoori oven (I bake it in my oven)—and a Bolognese-type sauce made with ground lamb and Indian spices. Thus was born a third favorite, which I christened "Naanizza"—a pizza in a sari. This improbable combination was so good that we still talk about it, and I think Queen Margherita of Savoy, the wife of King Umberto I of Italy, would not hold it against me. It is she we have to thank for the famous Pizza Margherita, which was created in her honor when she visited Naples in 1889; its red tomatoes, green basil, and white mozzarella topping represented the colors of the Italian flag. The only accompaniment the "Naanizza" needs is a green salad.

"Naanizza" (Spicy Lamb Naan Pizza)

Times

Active: 30 minutes
Rising: 1–1½ hours
Kneading: 12 minutes
Cooking: 25–30 minutes

Serves 12

Ingredients

For the naan dough
- 5½ cups (1 lb. 7 oz./650 g) all-purpose flour
- 1½ tsp salt
- 2 tbsp sugar
- 2 tbsp instant yeast
- 1 tbsp baking powder
- Scant 1 cup (220 ml) lukewarm milk
- 1 cup (9 oz./250 g) lightly beaten plain yogurt (see Notes)
- 2 eggs (see Notes)
- 3 tbsp peanut oil

For the lamb
- 3 onions
- 3 garlic cloves
- 1 bunch cilantro
- 1 bunch flat-leaf parsley
- 2 tbsp peanut oil
- 2 tbsp curry powder
- 1 tsp ground turmeric
- 1 tsp ground cinnamon
- 1 tbsp ground cumin
- 1 tsp ground ginger
- 1 small pinch Cayenne pepper
- 1⅔ cups (400 ml) plain tomato sauce
- 1 tbsp white vinegar
- 1¾ lb. (800 g) ground lamb from the leg
- Salt and freshly ground pepper

To prepare the naan dough, combine at low speed the flour, salt, sugar, yeast, and baking powder in the bowl of a stand mixer fitted with the dough hook. Add the lukewarm milk, yogurt, eggs, and peanut oil and knead for 10 minutes at medium speed, until the dough is smooth and elastic. Shape into a ball and transfer to a clean, lightly oiled bowl. Cover with plastic wrap and let rise for 1 hour at room temperature in a draft-free spot (a turned-off oven or a kitchen cabinet) until doubled in volume. An additional 30 minutes rising time may be necessary. Toward the end of the rising time, preheat the oven, with a baking sheet inside, to the highest possible temperature.

While the naan dough is rising, prepare the spicy lamb sauce. Peel and finely chop the onions and garlic, removing the germs from the garlic. Wash and dry the cilantro and parsley and chop the leaves finely. Coat one or two large skillets with the peanut oil and set over high heat. Add the onions and sauté for 3 minutes until softened, stirring occasionally. Add the spices, tomato sauce, vinegar, and lamb, breaking up any lumps of meat with a large fork to distribute the spices evenly. When the meat is cooked, add the garlic and herbs, simmering until most of the liquid has evaporated and the sauce is thick. Remove from the heat, taste, and add more spices or tomato sauce as needed.

To assemble the "Naanizza," once the dough has doubled in volume, knead it for 2 minutes to burst any air bubbles inside. Roll the dough out on a floured surface—or, even better, a silicone mat—to a thickness of ½ in. (1 cm) and brush the top with the melted butter. Remove the hot baking sheet from the oven, brush it with peanut oil, and carefully lift the dough onto it.

Spoon the lamb sauce evenly over the dough, sprinkle with the Parmesan, and bake for 10 minutes.

Scatter over the arugula and sprinkle with fleur de sel and freshly ground pepper. Serve at once, accompanied by a salad.

To assemble
- 1 tbsp melted butter
- Peanut oil, for greasing
- Generous ½ cup (2 oz./60 g) grated Parmesan

To garnish
- 3½ oz. (100 g) chopped arugula
- Fleur de sel
- Freshly ground pepper

Notes

To ensure a good rise, the eggs and yogurt must be at room temperature, so remember to take them out of the refrigerator 1 hour before making the dough.

Kesra (Moroccan Bread)

*The simplest, the quickest,
and the most delicious of breads.*

Times

Active: 15 minutes
Rising: 1 hour
Cooking: 25 minutes

Serves 12 (makes 2 loaves)
—

Ingredients

- Oil for greasing (or flour for dusting)
- 4 cups (1 lb./500 g) all-purpose flour, plus extra for dusting
- 1¾ cups (7 oz./200 g) whole wheat flour
- 1 tbsp salt
- 2 tbsp sugar
- 3½ tsp instant yeast
- 1½ cups (350 ml) lukewarm water
- 3 tbsp extra-virgin olive oil
- 2 tbsp sesame seeds, toasted in a skillet
- 2 tbsp flaxseeds, toasted in a skillet

Brush two 9½-in. (24-cm) round cake pans lightly with oil (or dust with flour). In the bowl of a stand mixer fitted with the dough hook, combine the flours, salt, sugar, and yeast for 30 seconds at low speed. Increase the speed to medium, gradually pour in the water, and knead for 5 minutes. Add the olive oil and seeds and knead for an additional 5 minutes, until the dough comes away completely from the sides of the bowl.

Transfer the dough to a dry, floured worktop—or, even better, a silicone mat. Cut it into two equal pieces and shape each piece into a smooth ball. Using the palm of your hand, flatten the balls into approximately 8-in. (20-cm) rounds, about ¾ in. (2 cm) thick.

Using a fork, pierce five deep sets of holes in a row across the center of each round, reaching all the way to the base. Dust the tops with a little flour and lift carefully into the prepared cake pans. Cover each one with a clean dish cloth and let rise at room temperature in a draft-free spot for 1 hour. After about 45 minutes, preheat the oven to 400°F (200°C/Gas mark 6) on fan setting and bake for 25 minutes, until the crust is crisp and golden. The bread is now ready and will smell wonderful!

Turn the loaves out onto a wire rack immediately and let cool. Then take a bite!

The Perfect Brioche

—

I have a gentleman in my life with whom I have tea every day, and I used to take great pride in offering him a selection of cakes such as financiers and madeleines. However, for a year now, when it's 4 p.m. and time for tea, all he wants is brioche. It's not easy finding good brioche, even ones made by respected bakers, as they can often be too dry, too greasy, or tasteless. So, I got to work and after umpteen attempts I've perfected two recipes that remind me of—can you guess?—the brioche of my childhood! This one is perfect for its texture, lightness, and flavor, and the aroma that fills the whole house when I bake it. It keeps well, too. Making brioche takes a bit of work, and a lot of time, but the rewards are infinite.

The Perfect Brioche

Times

Kneading: 20 minutes
Rising and proving: 4 hours–
  overnight
Cooking: 25 minutes

Serves 10

—

Ingredients

- 2¼ sticks (9 oz./250 g) diced
  butter (the best you can get),
  at room temperature, plus extra
  for greasing
- 4 cups (1 lb./500 g) all-purpose
  flour
- ½ cup (3½ oz./100 g) superfine
  sugar
- ½ oz. (15 g) fresh yeast,
  crumbled (or 1 tbsp instant
  yeast)
- 6 eggs
- 2 tsp fleur de sel

To glaze (optional)
- Beaten egg yolk and sugar

Grease a 5 × 10 in. (12 × 26 cm) loaf pan loaf pan with butter. In the bowl of a stand mixer fitted with the dough hook, mix together the flour, sugar, and yeast on high speed (without spattering yourself).

With the mixer still on high speed, add 1 pinch of the fleur de sel and four of the eggs. Reduce the speed to medium and add the two remaining eggs, one at a time, mixing the first in before adding the second. When the dough pulls away from the sides of the bowl, add the remaining fleur de sel and the butter. Continue mixing until the dough pulls away from the sides of the bowl again, but be patient—this will take a good 15 minutes. Turn the mixer off.

The dough will look silky, feel elastic, and be a pale-yellow color, which is just perfect! Cover the bowl with plastic wrap and let the dough rise at room temperature in a draft-free spot until doubled in volume (I put mine in the turned-off oven); you'll have a good 2 hours on your hands.

When the dough has doubled in volume, you will feel a great sense of satisfaction. To burst any air bubbles in it, punch the dough down four or five times and then pull and stretch it until it returns to its unrisen size. Place in a bowl, cover with plastic wrap, and refrigerate for at least 1 hour for it to rise and double in volume again.

Punch the dough down once more. You now have two choices. If you want to bake it that day, transfer the dough to the greased loaf pan, and let it prove until it doubles in volume, before baking according to the instructions below. Or, you can follow the advice of top pastry chef Pierre Hermé, who recommends covering the dough and placing it in the refrigerator overnight (it can also be frozen in an airtight container for up to one month). Let the dough come back to room temperature before baking.

The brioche can be baked plain or brushed with egg yolk and sprinkled with sugar. The oven needs to be very hot, so preheat it to 425°F (220°C/Gas mark 7) before baking the brioche for 25 minutes. If, after 15 minutes, it is already sufficiently brown, cover it with aluminum foil for the remaining cooking time.

Your brioche is done! Wait for 10 minutes before turning it out onto a cooling rack, and resist eating it hot!

Pear Loaf Cake

Moister than a quick bread and not as sweet as a layer cake, this pear loaf is a treat for all seasons and any time of the day. In summer, I use Bartlett pears, and in winter, Comice, but no matter when you make the cake, be sure to use the most fragrant and flavorful pears you can find. You can also replace some of the pears with apples, which will add extra texture and flavor, especially if you use slightly tart varieties like King of the Pippins or Belle de Boskoop. For a large number of guests, you can double the ingredients, dividing the batter between two loaf pans of the same size for even baking.

Times

Active: 30 minutes
Cooking: 55 minutes

Serves 8
—

Ingredients

- 7 tbsp (4 oz./110 g) salted butter, softened and divided, plus extra for greasing
- ¾ cup (3½ oz./110 g) all-purpose flour, plus extra for dusting
- 1¼ lb. (600 g) ripe pears, preferably Bartlett or Comice (depending on the time of year)
- Generous 1 tbsp honey
- Scant ⅔ cup (3 oz./90 g) confectioners' sugar
- 2 eggs
- ¾ tsp baking powder
- 1 pinch salt

To serve
- Green tea

Preheat the oven to 400°F (200°C/Gas mark 6). Grease a 9 × 5-in. (22 × 11-cm) loaf pan with butter, dust with flour, and set aside in the refrigerator. If you use a silicone pan, there is no need to grease, flour, or chill it.

Peel the pears and cut them into ¾-in. (2-cm) dice. Melt 2 tablespoons (1 oz./30 g) of the butter with the honey in a skillet over high heat. Add the pears and cook until they begin to turn golden, stirring constantly with two spatulas. When you smell caramel, remove the skillet from the heat.

Using an electric beater, whisk together the remaining butter and the sugar in a large bowl until creamy and light. Whisk in the eggs one at a time and, using a spatula, fold in the flour, baking powder, and salt until just combined. Carefully fold in the pears and then transfer the batter to the prepared pan.

Bake for 15 minutes. Lower the heat to 350°F (180°C/Gas mark 4) and bake for an additional 30 minutes, until a rich golden brown. If the top is browning too quickly, cover with aluminum foil or parchment paper. Let the cake cool in the pan for 15 minutes, then turn it out onto a wire rack.

Serve the cake warm with green tea—gyokuro and kuckicha from Japan are two I particularly like.

Luc's Crepes

—

Luc, my New Yorker grandson, absolutely adores these crepes—and he's not alone. Their soft, light texture and their flavor makes them truly exceptional and unlike anything called a crepe that you might have tasted before. Just roll them up like short, fat cigars and eat them as they are—they don't need any butter, honey, sugar, or jam. And they disappear in record time. I only make them once a year, in summer, when our family gathers from across the globe. Even though I start at dawn and no matter how many crepes I lovingly roll up (it was over one hundred last year with two skillets going at the same time), I always feel like I'm rationing them out. Who said desire was born from not enough to go around? As large amounts of the ingredients are required to make forty crepes, I recommend preparing the batter in two equal batches, using half the ingredients each time.

Luc's Crepes

Times

Active: 25 minutes
Cooking: 45 minutes

*Serves 10–12
(makes 40 crepes)*
—

Ingredients

- 1¾ sticks (7 oz./200 g) butter, plus 2 tbsp for greasing the skillets
- 4½ cups (1 liter) whole milk
- 8 eggs
- 1 pinch salt
- 1 cup (7 oz./200 g) sugar
- 1¾ cups (7 oz./200 g) pastry flour
- 1½ tsp Madagascan or Tahitian pure vanilla extract (or ground vanilla bean)

Prepare clarified butter by melting the 1¾ sticks (7 oz./200 g) butter gently over low heat in a heavy saucepan. Skim off the froth, then pour the clear yellow liquid into a pitcher, leaving behind the milky residue.

To make the batter, warm half the milk in a saucepan. Separate four of the eggs. Place the whites in the bowl of a stand mixer, sprinkle with a pinch of salt, and place the yolks in a separate large bowl. Sprinkle half the sugar over the yolks and whisk with an electric beater until pale and thick. Whisk in half the flour, half the clarified butter, and half the vanilla. Add the warmed milk in a thin stream and continue whisking until smooth.

Beat the egg whites until they hold soft peaks, then lightly fold them into the batter, which should be frothy and thick. Make a second batch of batter in the same way, using the remaining ingredients.

To cook the crepes, use one or two 8-in. (20-cm) nonstick skillets or crepe pans. Melt the 2 tablespoons of butter in one skillet and pour it into a bowl—you'll use it for greasing between each crepe. Set your skillet(s) over medium-high heat and brush with a little of the melted butter. With a spoon that holds about 2 tablespoons of liquid, but no more, scoop out batter from the bottom of the bowl to the top (the top is mainly froth). Pour into each skillet, swirling to coat the base. After a few seconds, the crepe should have bubbles on the surface, be golden underneath, and pale on top—it's cooked. Using a wooden spatula (preferably angled), gently roll the crepe toward you to make a loose scroll and transfer to a plate. Don't worry—it may take a few tries to get the hang of it. Between each crepe, brush the skillet(s) with a little more melted butter and cook more crepes until you've used all the batter. Stack the rolled crepes on a serving plate as you go. Serve hot, as they are.

Notes

You can make the batter and cook the crepes several hours in advance. To reheat them, microwave them on the serving plate on full power for about 2 minutes, until hot. Serve at once.

Perfect Madeleines

Among "ordinary" things that are anything but, madeleines rival the omelet. I tried umpteen recipes before settling on Joël Robuchon's mini honey madeleines, which became my favorite for years. They are exquisite but tiny—just right for accompanying ice cream or a good cup of coffee. These regular-sized madeleines are perfect on their own and the recipe is simple and practical. The batter keeps for up to three days in the refrigerator and is optimal if you make it at least one day ahead for airy and delicious madeleines that take just twelve minutes to bake. They are best eaten warm, so only bake the quantity you need—they don't keep well, even in an airtight container. Keep any leftover batter covered in the fridge and bake it the following day, so you can once again enjoy the aroma and flavor of freshly baked madeleines.

Times

Make 2 hours or a day ahead
Active: 15 minutes
Resting: 2 hours (or preferably 24 hours)
Cooking: 12 minutes

Makes about 30

Ingredients

- 1 cup plus 1 tbsp (5 oz./140 g) all-purpose flour
- 2 tsp baking powder
- 3 tbsp cocoa powder (optional; use for chocolate madeleines variation)
- 1 stick plus 2 tbsp (5¼ oz./150 g) salted butter
- 3 tbsp milk
- 1 tbsp honey
- 1 pinch Madagascan or Tahitian ground vanilla bean
- 2 eggs
- ½ cup (3½ oz./100 g) sugar
- Melted butter or oil, for greasing

Sift the flour and baking powder (and cocoa powder, if making chocolate madeleines) into a medium bowl. Clarify the butter by melting it gently over low heat in a heavy saucepan. Skim off the froth, then pour the clear yellow liquid into a pitcher, leaving behind the milky residue. In a separate saucepan, warm the milk, honey, and vanilla over low heat. Beat the eggs and sugar together in a mixing bowl until pale and foamy and a thick ribbon falls from the beaters when the whisk is lifted. Lightly fold in the warm milk mixture, followed by the sifted flour mixture and clarified butter until the mixture is evenly combined. Press plastic wrap against the surface and refrigerate for 24 hours (ideally), or at least 2 hours.

Half an hour before serving, preheat the oven to 350°F (180°C/ Gas mark 4). Generously grease cavities in regular madeleine pans with melted butter or oil, according to the number you wish to bake. Stir the batter until smooth and then fill the molds using two small spoons: one containing the batter and the other for pushing it into each cavity. Bake for 12 minutes, until golden, let cool for 2 minutes in the pans, and then serve at once. You can either turn the madeleines out onto a serving plate or—the chic option—serve them directly from the pan (having released them first with a knife), taking care not to burn yourself.

Theo's Meringues

It's amazing how many people—children and adults alike—love meringues, but nobody likes them as much as Theo, my Californian grandson. When he was little (he's now fifteen and wears a size thirteen shoe), nothing made me happier than to catch him and his little brother Zach with their hands in the meringue jar. The half-guilty, half-joyful look on Theo's face was priceless.

Times

Active: 10 minutes
Cooking: 2 hours

Makes about 30 egg-size meringues

—

Ingredients

- 4 egg whites
- ⅔ cup (4½ oz./125 g) superfine sugar
- 1 cup (4½ oz./125 g) confectioners' sugar

Preheat the oven to 200°F (100°C/Gas mark ¼) and line two baking sheets with silicone baking mats or parchment paper.

Using an electric beater, whisk the egg whites on high speed until soft peaks form. Whisk in the superfine sugar a little at a time, continuing to whisk for 4–5 minutes, until the whites are stiff and shiny.

Quickly fold in the confectioners' sugar using a wooden spatula, until evenly combined.

Shape the meringues using two tablespoons if, like me, you'd rather not use a pastry bag. Fill one spoon with meringue, level it off and slide the meringue onto a lined baking sheet with the second spoon. Continue until you've used all the meringue mixture, leaving ¾ in. (2 cm) between each one. Bake for 2 hours until the meringues are dry and crisp.

Take the meringues out of the oven and, when cool enough to handle, gently remove them from the mats or parchment paper. Store in an old-fashioned candy jar or a metal cookie tin, but wait until they have been out of the oven for at least 30 minutes before sealing the jar or tin or you risk the meringues going soft. They will keep for 3–4 weeks—as long as Theo is not around.

Notes

If this is your first attempt at making meringues, I suggest halving the ingredients for a practice run. Soon, like me, you'll be doubling them, much to the delight of all those you know with a sweet tooth.

Caramelized Apple Pascade

Unique, wonderfully fluffy, and easy to make, this pascade—a large oven-puffed crepe, similar to a Dutch baby pancake, from the French department of Aveyron—makes a good base for its topping of delicious caramelized apples. Lighter and quicker to prepare than a tart, it's a delightful treat. If you can get King of the Pippins apples in the fall, you'll be richly rewarded. Otherwise, I'll let you in on a chef's secret: combine three different varieties to boost the apple flavor.

Times
Active: 30 minutes
Cooking: 30 minutes

Serves 8
—

Ingredients

For the pascade
- Butter, for greasing
- 1 orange
- ⅔ cup (150 ml) whole milk
- 2 eggs
- 4 tbsp sugar
- 1½ tbsp brown sugar
- ½ cup (2 oz./60 g) all-purpose flour

For the topping
- 3½ lb. (1.5 kg) King of the Pippins or Belle de Boskoop apples (or 3 different varieties)
- ½ cup (3½ oz./100 g) brown sugar
- 2 tbsp salted butter

To garnish
- Sliced almonds or sesame seeds

To serve (optional)
- Whipped cream or Crème Anglaise (see recipe p. 193)

Preheat the oven to 350°F (180°C/4). Grease a 9-in. (22-cm) tart pan or oven-safe skillet, at least 2 in. (5 cm) deep, with butter.

To prepare the *pascade* batter, wash and dry the orange, finely grate the zest, and squeeze the juice. In a large bowl, whisk together the milk, eggs, orange juice, zest, sugar, and brown sugar for 1 minute. Add the flour and whisk until you have a smooth batter.

Pour the batter into the prepared pan—the batter should be 1¼–1½ in. (3–4 cm) deep—and bake for 25–30 minutes, until puffed and golden.

Meanwhile, prepare the topping. Peel and core the apples. Grate them on the large holes of a box grater.

In a large skillet, melt the brown sugar by swirling pan over high heat, add the butter and stir until melted. Add the apples and sauté for 3–4 minutes, tossing with two spatulas until lightly caramelized. Keep warm.

When the *pascade* is cooked, remove it from the oven and turn it out onto a serving plate. Pile the warm apples on top, shaping them into a dome. Sprinkle with sliced almonds or sesame seeds and serve immediately, with or without whipped cream or, if you prefer, Crème Anglaise.

indexes

Recipes by Title

Recipes by Ingredient

Recipes by Season

Recipes by Type of Dish

Recipes by Time to Make

Recipes by Country

Vegetarian Recipes

Certain recipes may contain eggs, milk, butter, or honey.

Gluten-Free Recipes

All recipes in this book can be made gluten-free with the following substitutions:

Acknowledgments

- To our precious Édith Mezard, from the Château de l'Ange in Lumières, for her plates (page 42). Her place is an oasis of refinement and temptations that we frequently fail to resist.

- To my Roulades—my friends who are crazy about food—who assisted and supported me throughout this performance in the midst of a Provençal heat wave: forty dishes in four days!

- To Nathalie Carnet, the photographer, whose good humor was boundless, including the four retakes it took to photograph the Zach's Chocolate Truffle Cake.

- To Lurdès who assisted me efficiently in the kitchen.

- To Philippe, the vegetable garden master.

- To JL, my husband, whose patience was infinite.